The Science of Spelling

The Science of Spelling

The Explicit Specifics That Make Great Readers and Writers (and Spellers!)

J. Richard Gentry, Ph.D.

HEINEMANN

Portsmouth, NH

Heinemann
A division of Reed Elsevier Inc.
361 Hanover Street
Portsmouth, NH 03801–3912
www.heinemann.com

Offices and agents throughout the world

The author and publisher wish to thank those who have generously given permission to reprint borrowed material:

Appendix A, Table 1: Adaptation of Developmental Spelling Test Scoring Chart from "You Can Analyze Developmental Spelling" by J. Richard Gentry. Reprinted with permission of the publisher, Early Years, Inc. From the May 1985 issue of *Teaching K–8 Magazine*, Norwalk, CT 06854.

Figures 5–1, 5–2, 5–3, 5–5, 5–10, and "Grade 3 Pre-Test": From *Spell It-Write! Spelling Process Handbook* by J. Richard Gentry. Copyright © 1998 by J. Richard Gentry. Reprinted by permission of Zaner-Bloser, Inc.

Figure 5–6: Adapted from "Spelling Strategies" by J. Richard Gentry. First published in *Instructor* (p. 77), September 1997. New York: Scholastic.

"The Writing Scale" and "Techniques Defined" adapted from "Instructional Techniques for Emerging Writers and Special Needs Students at Kindergarten and Grade 1 Levels" from *Reading & Writing Quarterly* (in press to be published in Vol. 21, No. 2, April 2005) by J. Richard Gentry. Philadelphia, PA: Taylor Francis.

Library of Congress Cataloging-in-Publication Data
Gentry, J. Richard.
   The science of spelling : the explicit specifics that make great readers and writers (and spellers!) / J. Richard Gentry.
      p. cm.
   Includes bibliographical references and index.
   ISBN 0-325-00717-9 (alk. paper)
   1. Spelling ability. 2. English language—Orthography and spelling. 3. Reading. I. Title

LB1574.G37 2004   2004011230
372.63'2—dc22

Editor: Lois Bridges
Production service: Denise Botelho
Production coordination: Vicki Kasabian
Cover design: Jenny Jensen Greenleaf
Author photograph: Barbara Marker
Typesetter: TechBooks, Inc.
Manufacturing: Steve Bernier

Printed in the United States of America on acid-free paper
08 07 06 05   EB   2 3 4 5

For Bill,

And for Bonnie and Miriam

Contents

Acknowledgments

It was a brief encounter but such a gracious and kind invitation from Lois Bridges, the superb editor at Heinemann, that set this book in motion. I had been working for two years on the concept when Lois walked up to me in the lobby of the Peabody Hotel, gave me a note with her email address, and invited me to send her my next book. Lois received my manuscript six months later and worked her magic. I am grateful for her talent, for the work of Heinemann's Editorial Coordinator, Karen Clausen, Vicki Kasabian Production Editor, and production services by Denise Botelho, as well as the other fine staff at Heinemann who are dedicated to providing books of the highest quality for teachers.

I am grateful to have been a graduate student of Edmund H. Henderson at the University of Virginia, and to be a part of "the spelling club," a group of Ed's students who have worked diligently for many years to follow Ed's legacy and improve the teaching of spelling and literacy. Ed once sent me a letter describing a spelling presentation I had done as "an absolute bombshell. It was simply Venus out of the head of Zeus— the (spelling) findings spontaneously revealed in a living child." His words inspired me to work with this topic for over twenty years. I owe a debt of gratitude to Ed and to his life's work.

I go to my bookshelf and in one section of prized volumes I see the names of powerful contemporary educational researchers who have helped shape my thinking: Yetta and Ken Goodman, Regie Routman, Marilyn Adams, Dorothy Strickland, Richard Allington, Marie Clay, Irene Fountas, Gay Su Pinnell, Don Graves, Nancie Atwell, Pat Cunningham, Richard Hodges, Ronald Cramer, Margaret Peters, Steve Graham, Charles Read, Jerry Zutell, Shane Templeton, Donald Bear, Tim Rasinski, Charles Temple, Mary Jo Fresch, Kathy Ganske, Darrell Morris, Jean Gillet, Tom Gill, and so many others. Sometimes it was the dissenting view that challenged me to think deeper and clarify my own thinking and I am grateful to Katie Wood Ray, Lester Laminack, and others who may not have agreed with my perspective.

If you read this book, you will see how important and powerful research by Connie Juel, Linnea Ehri, Linda Allal, Elena Bodrova, Deborah Leong, Eileen Feldgus, Isabell Cardonick, as well as the work of the neuroscientists, such as Sally Shaywitz, who conducted the brain scan studies, influenced my thinking. I am grateful to these researchers for their contributions to education and literacy.

I spend a great deal of time working in schools with children. I am most grateful to those children who shared literacy experiences with me. I learn so much from my observations and conversations with children.

I have been privileged to work with some of the best teachers and administrators in America. Thank you to Bill McIntyre, Judy Farley, Penny Jamaison, Gert Johnson, Earl Watson, Lilia Nanez, Dalia Benavides, Patty Baxter, Paula Eggleston, Ceil Aiken, Carolyn Miegs, and so many others.

A special thank you to Beverly Kingery and Richard Craddock, two fine, intelligent educators and talented colleagues whom I admire. They read parts of my manuscript and offered suggestions and encouragement. Many thanks also to Sandra Wilde, who read the entire manuscript and was gracious, insightful, and generous in her encouragement, offering many specific suggestions that went into this book.

Bill Boswell inspired me, gave me important ideas, and worked constantly to help me with this project and to make my life great. I am deeply thankful.

Writing is sometimes lonely work. There were times when I was isolated, tethered to my computer, working on holidays or late into the night, and a sixteen-pound fuzzy cat tiptoed in, sneaked under the desk, gave me a nudge, and planted his huge mound of orange fur at my feet just to keep me company. Thanks Mies.

The Science of Spelling

Is there new biological evidence for giving spelling education more status, and for teaching spelling explicitly?

1

Discovery #1: There Is a Neurological Basis for Spelling

In spring of 1988, I was standing on the floor of the exhibit hall at the International Reading Association's International Convention in Toronto, chatting with two world-renown language arts researchers about spelling. Awestruck to be in their company, I found them more than gracious to share their ideas. Both had read my book, *Spel . . . Is a Four-Letter Word* (1987), and these giants among reading researchers encouraged me "to keep up the good work."

At one point in our discussion, one of them made a statement that startled me: "Richard," she said, "there's no such thing as a spelling disability!" The researcher was brilliant in her knowledge of reading and spelling research, passionate in her conviction, and eloquent in her ability to cite numerous research studies off the top of her head. She challenged my own firmly held belief that, due to an internal processing difficulty, many children and adults, including myself, could not spell well. My hunch was that expert spelling was hardwired and there was a glitch in my own circuitry for spelling. The distinguished researcher averred this was proven false and referred me to studies in countries like Italy, where children don't have spelling problems. Then she stated the cutting-edge, research-based view on this topic during that era: *If whole nations exist where people who are literate in alphabetic languages have no spelling disability, then spelling disability cannot be neurologically based.* It followed that if spelling is culture-specific and variable across countries, we should soft-pedal spelling instruction. This belief was underpinned by educational theory that was growing in popularity: Children learn to spell by reading, it was thought—spelling need not be taught explicitly (Smith 1971). The popular view was that spelling knowledge would be "caught" as children immersed themselves in reading and writing. Academic focus on spelling was of relatively little importance for literacy learning. Spelling instruction was a literacy glamour shot—pretty to look at but limited in substance. Of course, it was deemed important to teach a few basic spelling principles, but teachers might easily teach spelling during reading and writing instruction in demonstrations and minilessons. They might simply anticipate what minilessons might be needed, wait for teachable moments, and without spending a lot of time or using boring spelling books, teach spelling "off the top of the head" as children used it in their writing (Laminack and Wood 1996). Whole states adopted these beliefs, and many teachers stopped teaching spelling directly. In California, the state department of education banned spelling books from the required textbook list.

The neurological issue was just one of the spelling issues that have huge implications for teaching and learning literacy. The researcher's position challenged my beliefs not only about that issue, but also about the complexity of spelling and the importance of teaching spelling explicitly. On the reality of spelling disability, my convictions were strong and personal. The idea that spelling disability didn't exist seemed off base—I was pretty sure I had one!

My own spelling disability has been a life-long challenge. As a struggling speller, my diligence to eradicate this problem, followed by a career built on spelling and literacy research, convinced me that, somehow, parts of the research view of that time were misguided. Something in my brain just did not click for spelling, and I doubted I was the only one whose brain froze up when they tried to see a word in their mind. As a teacher, reading professor, researcher, and director of a university reading center, I had worked with hundreds of school-age children whose difficulties with spelling seemed much like my own, and in my view, these difficulties seemed to be neurologically based. It became my quest to help teachers understand spelling and resolve the reality of the spelling disability issue as well as other important issues surrounding spelling and the teaching of literacy.

My search was driven in part by worry that since the 1970s, a whole generation of children in America may have been disenfranchised from spelling instruction because authorities told teachers that children learn to spell by reading; consequently, many children grew up without spelling instruction. I was also skeptical about the "spelling is caught from reading" theory because it was dreadfully disappointing for me. I read a lot, and assuming that the theory worked, I should have become a fairly good speller. Instead, the more words I read and the larger my reading and speaking vocabularies grew, the greater the number of words I could misspell!

The school-age generation of the 1950s through the 1970s—my generation—faired equally poorly with spelling. It was a time of poorly designed spelling books, mindless spelling book exercises, and very little instruction. Spelling was tested but not taught.

I have clear recollection of my own struggles with spelling. The spelling book I used in elementary school was abominable—a collection of inane exercises devoid of the information I needed to spell with accuracy. I was brilliant at solving the exercises but miserable at spelling with correctness. Even then, I was clever enough to recognize that circling all the list words beginning with th and sounding like /th/ in *thin* and underlining all list words beginning with th and sounding like /th/ as in *then* had nothing to do with their spelling. Voiced or unvoiced, they were all spelled th.

Instruction in spelling was not part of my elementary school experience. Spelling was assigned but not taught. There was a book, exercises, assignments, and tests, but not teaching, and I struggled and memorized but had little understanding of how English spelling worked. The patterns and consistency of English spelling escaped me.

There was an unending emphasis on grading during my elementary years, and I gave the teachers what they wanted. I had a perfect record of spelling achievement: all *As* in spelling in every grade in elementary school; a personal record of 252 "one hundreds" on the Friday spelling test in second through eighth grade.

Week after week, I made 100 percent on the spelling test. My record of one hundreds masked my word knowledge ignorance. Faking out my teachers was easy, but remembering perfect spellings was impossible! For seven years I masqueraded as genius of the spelling book exercises and champion of memorization for the test. In fact, I was a pitiful speller—and I knew it.

In seventh grade I memorized over 1,600 words on a spelling list to win my elementary school spelling bee, only to forget many of the spellings in a short time. (I was number three in the district and won a plaque.) Despite my hard work, I entered high school a lousy speller with a stunning record of extremely high spelling achievement, and I appalled my ninth grade English teacher when I misspelled *grammar* in my first high school English paper.

My heroic spelling improvement efforts stretched into adulthood. I became an expert on phonics and volunteered to teach the phonics course in my university department until the faculty banned the course when phonics instruction "went out." My command of spelling rules and word pattern minutia was extraordinary. Understanding completely that being a good speller was more complex than memorizing words, I studied and tried every spelling improvement strategy imaginable. While my spelling improved, my spelling accuracy was staggeringly pathetic, a liability at my level of education.

After chatting at the convention with the distinguished researchers, I longed to discover if my hunch were correct: Expert speller's "see words" in their minds—poor spellers cannot see them. Are respective brain circuitries in good spellers and poor spellers different?

The search for neurological proof of the causes of spelling disability has taken over fifteen years. I have had to wait for a convergence of medical science and educational theory and practice. I believe research results are now at a stage at which they can be applied. In this chapter, I'll report some important findings in the intervening years and then share what I consider to be the proof, along with important educational implications for teaching literacy brought on by this discovery.

In the last ten years, I found research that hinted at a neurological basis for spelling, and studies that skirted the edge of the issue. For example, I found fascinating work by Utta Frith and her colleagues that encouraged serious study of spelling and suggested that some sort of visual coding mechanism might exist for storing words in the brain as spellings. This work made sense, given my experience. My "visual coding mechanism" wasn't working!

Then there was Marilyn Adams' influential work, *Beginning to Read: Thinking and Learning about Print*, in 1990. She maintained that readers do not simply sample the text but look at virtually all the letters in a word and nearly every word in a sentence during skilled reading. Furthermore, she reported that the brain processed letters in words almost instantaneously into recognizable patterns. Her explanation sounded to me surprisingly close to neurologically based spelling. If it were true that the brain processes *letters in words*, I surmised, spelling may be more important for reading and literacy than we realize.

Early on, Ed Henderson, my major professor in the doctoral program at the University of Virginia, recognized the importance of spelling for reading that was going against the grain of the cutting edge research view of his day. He described how the emerging reader's development of a concept of word, use of finger pointing, and concurrent development and use of invented spellings aided the acquisition of reading ability. Ed recognized that words are understood as complete entities. He viewed the ability to identify words in text, or concept of word, as a watershed event in enabling young children to focus their attention on word units so that the printed word "stood alone" for the child's analysis. Once a child knew what a spoken and printed word was, Ed surmised, it was easier to figure out how its letters map to its sounds. Then the child could "break the code" by deciphering how the alphabetic system works, which in turn made it possible to read ([1985]1990). As the child integrated concept of word with knowledge of invented spelling by performing operations such as playing with rhyming words, segmenting sounds in words, and discovering what letters or chunks of letters could be used to invent spellings, it was easier for the child to read or write, and perhaps easier to retrieve words from memory. While other researchers were downsizing spelling instruction, Henderson upgraded its importance due to this powerful reading–spelling connection.

Henderson's ideas foreshadowed a groundbreaking discovery by Linnea Ehri in 1997: *Learning to read and learning to spell are almost the same process!* Ehri's comprehensive description of how word knowledge develops in the beginning reader included descriptions of phases of word recognition meshing exactly with stages of invented spelling. There were four developmental levels observed independently by both reading researchers and spelling researchers in developing readers and developing spellers. Reading researchers and spelling researchers seemed to be observing the same process: Knowledge of the alphabetic system differed at each level, how children operated differed at each level, and the approach that predominated changed at each level. Furthermore, descriptions of what was happening with reading and spelling within each of the four levels were astonishingly similar. The progression from Level 1 through Level 4 moved along a continuum, typically in kindergarten through first grade, toward eventual skilled reading and spelling. Ultimately, it was a progression culminating when the child broke the code and fully grasped how the alphabetic system worked in all its complexity. Invented spelling, a snapshot of what was happening in the child's mind during this time, told an indisputable story of how early spelling and word knowledge developed. It was a story of shifts in what children paid attention to and in what they ignored (Ehri 1997, 261). Of course, there were individual differences, with some children developing faster or slower, but for the most part, the story was consistent. In studies of early reading and spelling, researchers were seeing tangible evidence in children's productions of shifts in their thinking. Their invented spellings left a footprint of how they thought the alphabet system worked, and the footprints changed in form as the inventive spellers moved toward increasingly more sophisticated understandings of how orthography works. These footprints left an indelible record of the child's thinking. Take out the memorized spellings, and four levels of writing emerged generally from kindergarten to the end of first grade:

Level 1: GPDHGKRDH (Usually first half of kindergarten)

Level 2: WZ HRD 2 RD. (Usually second half of kindergarten)

Level 3: DA UZD WON LATTR FR EVRE SOND. (Usually first half of first grade)

Level 4: OFFUN THAY YOUSED THEE RONG PATURNS. (Usually second half of first grade)

At the beginning of the year, kindergartners likely started invented spellings using letters, but they ignored the sounds in words. There were no letter–sound matches, and writing looked like strings of random letters. The students were spelling at Level 1.

About mid-kindergarten, inventive spellers shifted to paying particular attention to prominent sounds in the words they were spelling, and they matched the sound with an appropriate letter, producing spellings such as BT for *bat*. Medial sounds were largely ignored. These partial alphabetic representations were Level 2.

Spellers shifted again, often in the middle of first grade, to Level 3, using a concrete strategy—a letter for each sound in a word. While one could read everything they wrote in this fashion, the words they invented were unconventional. (In English, a letter for a sound doesn't work!) Interestingly, these Level 3 spellers might read word families with ease, paying attention to the patterns, but ignore the same spelling patterns when they wrote. Just as reading a word is easer than spelling a word, recognizing the pattern is a lot easier than producing it.

As shifts in spelling inventions are taking place, children produce a few correct spellings automatically—their names and words such as *cat* and *love*. Initially, they don't seem to have a clue why the words are spelled as they are. The invented spelling, however, tells the story of what they really know about spelling at a particular stage in development, and it shows their changing concept of how the English system works.

Finally, beginning spellers shifted to a level where they represented sounds in words as chunks of phonics patterns. From the middle to end of first grade, they typically shifted to Level 4, consolidating their growing understanding of phonics, as they shifted from one letter for a sound to using chunks of phonics patterns. They began to use our curious English system of marking particular sound features visually, not just a letter for a sound, but a silent *e* to make the vowel long, in a pattern such as CVCe, for example (*make, Pete, bite, note, cute*). This shift to using patterns brought about the use of other letter chunks and combinations, demonstrating the speller's growing knowledge of phonics.

Emerging readers clearly comprehended the spelling of a word in these four unfolding stages, which co-occurred with reading phases and ended, with the exception of Level 4, as they learned to read seamlessly at about seven years of age. The co-occurrences of levels for phases of reading and stages of spelling are represented in Figure 1–1. I studied these changing shifts in invented spelling and contemplated Ehri's almost identical phases of word learning, and I wondered if brain research might reveal new regions of the brain becoming activated as children advanced through developmental levels.

For me, the Ehri study showed a reading–spelling connection that made sense in regard to my synthesis of research, my observations of what children do in the classroom and clinic, and my own personal experience as a speller. But Ehri took her observations a step further. After

LEVELS		
Shifts in Thinking or Changes in Focus	Ehri's (1997) Phases of Word Reading	Gentry's (2000b) Stages of Spelling
Level 1	Pre-alphabetic	Precommunicative
Level 2	Partial alphabetic	Semiphonetic
Level 3	Full alphabetic	Phonetic
Level 4	Consolidated alphabetic	Transitional

FIGURE 1–1   **Different Levels of Knowledge of the Alphabetic System**

showing that learning to read and learning to spell are mutually facilitative and reciprocal, she made two landmark conclusions:

- "Students need explicit spelling instruction as well as explicit reading instruction."
- Spelling skill should not be acquired through reading instruction. (265)

In formulating the beginning reading–spelling connection, Ehri inferred that "the reason why spelling helps reading is that spelling instruction helps to cultivate students' knowledge of the alphabetic system which benefits processes used in reading" (261). It was direct support for the Henderson hypothesis. And like Henderson's idea, Ehri's observation that spelling helps reading went against the grain of the prevailing research-based view at the time of her study. Before Henderson and Ehri, spelling had toppled from the instructional pedestal. It seemed to me that Ehri was re-erecting spelling instruction as one of the pillars of learning to read.

In my view, Ehri's work touched on the neurological issue—not in any direct way, but by giving spelling legitimacy and instructional prominence. She disavowed the "children learn to spell by reading" idea. Perhaps inadvertently, she put spelling, if not in the driver's seat, at least in the engine for driving emergent literacy. How different from the prevailing view that teaching spelling explicitly was not important for becoming literate.

During the fifteen years of my search, Connie Juel made extraordinary contributions in helping me understand beginning reading. Her research implications for focusing on the type and timing of instruction during beginning levels coupled well with the phases and stages findings (Juel 1994). I began to think about instruction that would *lead* children from one phase or stage to the next higher level, an idea that resonated with the teachings of Vygotsky (1978). This work is described more fully in Chapter 3.

Another powerful understanding with important implications clearly implied in both Ehri's and Juel's work is the difference between *becoming* a reader–speller (i.e., beginning or emergent reading) and *being* a skilled reader–speller, which often happens by the end of first grade. I began to look at *beginning reading and spelling* and *skilled reading and spelling* separately. The "spelling is caught from reading" theory drew implications for teaching beginners based on observation of what skilled readers–spellers do. What if learning to read and spell versus reading and spelling automatically were different processes. Understanding the dynamics of *beginning* versus *skilled* reading/spelling might become clearer when the initial learning of the process was viewed independently from the skilled implementation of it. The type and timing of teaching strategies for those who were learning the processes might be different than instruction that was needed to move already skilled readers and spellers to higher levels of sophistication. What if the brain activation were different for readers–spellers who were beginning versus readers–spellers who were skilled? If spelling were, in fact, part biological and we could see how the brain worked, we might be closer to understanding spelling and its true connection to literacy development.

The baffling problem of the variance in spelling disability from country to country remained unsolved until 2001. Why is it that the United States, France, and Great Britain have lots of struggling spellers and Italy has relatively few? The tantalizing question was still open: Were spelling problems culture-specific or biologically based?

The answer has resulted from a convergence of medical research and educational inquiry. In the early 1980s, magnetic resonance imaging (MRI) made it possible for neuroscientists not only to see the human brain's structure but also, for the first time, to see the brain's *function* during cognitive processes such as thinking, speaking, and reading. Using a technology called positron emission tomography (PET), scientists could use brain scans to see the brain's activity by measuring the blood flow in various cerebral regions. The early studies involved injecting radioactive compounds into the bloodstream intravenously and recording the regional distribution of radioactivity. Local blood flow in specific areas of the brain was found to increase when that area was functioning. PET scans made it possible for the researchers to chart the sequence of events in various parts of the brain as subjects engaged in various linguistic tasks. Ultimately, the studies revealed three (some studies report four) major "reading areas" of the brain that performed various functions during reading and reading-related processes. One of the areas showed language linked to visual cues, which, for our purposes, I call "the spelling area." It has long been theorized that a spelling area existed separate from the primary reading areas because brain injuries in literate adults may result in their loss of reading ability while their spelling ability remains intact, or vice versa.

In the spring of 2001, a study entitled "Dyslexia: Cultural Diversity and Biological Unity" (Paulesu et al. 2001) was published, in which researchers used PET scans to determine if dyslexia were a neurodevelopmental disorder. The study was of particular interest to me as a spelling researcher because severe spelling disability accompanies signs of dyslexia. I've never heard of a true dyslexic who spells well. Researchers from Italy, France, and Great Britain used the brain scan technique to study dyslexic and normal readers from the three countries. They were looking for the roots of dyslexia. Were the roots biological or cultural? Italy definitely had far fewer people with reading problems than the United States, Great Britain, and France, but what was the reason?

Seventy-two males with tertiary education participated in the brain scan study—twenty-four from each country, half of them normal readers and half of them dyslexic as determined by clinical tests. Brain activation data were collected on these normal and dyslexic readers. Interestingly, all brain regions associated with reading showed greater activation for normal subjects than for dyslexics. Another important finding was that dyslexic subjects produced different brain scan profiles than did normal subjects. Even though Italian dyslexics were far better readers than were the French or English dyslexics, the brain functions of all three dyslexic groups were similar. Certain brain areas in all dyslexics were inactive during the reading task, no matter what language they spoke. *The main inactive area was one that scientists report to link language to visual cues.* Was this boundary between language and visual processing the same area enabling expert spellers to "see spelling in their mind's eye?" During reading, the normal brains were reported to be active in three areas linking the visual cues of the language to sound and meaning (Kher 2001, 56). Remarkably, the dyslexic brains did not respond in the visual cue areas of printed language. Were the visual cue areas where normal readers store representations of *spellings*? It's plausible, because expert spellers report their ability to "see the word in their minds" while poor spellers don't see the words. Poor spellers report that they can't see the words, so

English	Italian
44 sounds	25 sounds
1,120 spelling combinations for these sounds	33 spelling combinations for these sounds

FIGURE 1–2   Comparison of English and Italian Orthography

their strategy is to spell them like they sound. This study led me to conclude that there are two clinical differences in the spelling ability of normal versus dyslexic readers:

1. Normal readers use an area of the brain that helps them see words in their minds.
2. Dyslexics, who do learn to read, do not activate the visual cue area, and they neither see words in their minds nor spell well.

Because poor spelling is a telltale sign of dyslexia, I interpret Paulesu and his colleague's dyslexia study also to be one of normal spellers versus disabled spellers, showing a neurological basis for their differences. At a minimum, the study suggests possible neurological connections to causes of spelling problems in severely disabled spellers, because extremely poor spelling virtually always accompanies dyslexia by most definitions of the disorder.

Accounting for the discrepancy between the number of dyslexics in countries like the United States and Italy isn't the only important spelling connection in the study. Why were the Italian dyslexic subjects far better readers than the English and French dyslexics, even though their brain functions were similar? It turned out that reading Italian takes a lot less effort because of its spelling. There's a big difference in the orthography or the spelling system of the languages. Italian has a much easier spelling system than English or French, and that apparently facilitates reading to the extent that Italian dyslexics might not even know they were dyslexic unless they took psychological tests to confirm it. The differences in the spelling systems are stunning. As depicted in Figure 1–2, English has more than a thousand different ways to spell its forty-four sounds. Italian has twenty-five sounds and only thirty-three different ways to spell them (Kher 2001, 56). With this staggering contrast, it is no wonder that Italians are great spellers.

I consider the Paulesu study to be another watershed event for our understanding of spelling. The researchers' biologically based findings of "a universal neurocognitive basis for dyslexia" may be interpreted to provide direct evidence of a neurological basis for spelling disability. Subsequent studies reported later in this book provide further support for this interpretation: *There is a neurological basis for spelling.*

Implications

The implications from the discovery of a neurological base for spelling are powerful. They can be summarized in three guidelines for teaching.

1. Put spelling on a pedestal.

The discovery of a neurological basis for spelling is important because it turns our previous idea about the reading–spelling connection on its head, even suggesting that we flip-flop the *children learn to spell by reading* theory. It's more accurate to say that *children learn to read by spelling!* What I am suggesting is that early spelling knowledge is what enables children to learn the alphabetic principle or, in essence, break the code for reading, and this knowledge can be taught in appropriate spelling instruction. Although reading is certainly multifaceted and complex, breaking the code is a necessary if not sufficient condition for success with reading. No one can read well without breaking the code: *Spelling* is the Rosetta Stone of that process. With the beginner, as spelling knowledge unfolds, so, too, does the knowledge needed for success with reading. When we *teach* the knowledge needed for spelling to the beginning reader—knowledge about sounds, letter knowledge, concept of what a word is, phonemic awareness, knowledge of the alphabetic principle for mapping spoken language to its printed form, knowledge of spelling patterns (i.e., phonics), and how phonics brings some pattern and consistency to a very complex system for mapping printed language to spoken language—we are teaching the underlying knowledge needed for reading, and for writing. Instead of saying that spelling instruction is not important, we should say that it is. Even in the most talked-about metaanalysis of reading research in the last decade in the United States, *The Report of the National Reading Panel,* funded by the federal government, encompassing reading researchers and educators from across the country, spelling was not adequately addressed (2000). Of course, spelling is in the study—as "phonemic awareness," as "phonics," as aspects of "fluency," and in other guises—but it's never really called by its name: It's *spelling!* Spelling is not everything important for reading, but in the coming chapters, I argue that spelling unlocks the first vault of literacy, leading to deeper vaults for words, for fluency, and for meaning. Meaning comes first in language, but to get to meaning in language's printed from, it makes sense to begin with spelling.

2. Teach spelling explicitly.

We now know how to teach spelling, and I will try to show you what we know in a straightforward and practical manner. What we know about how to teach spelling has changed. For the first time, the research results are at a stage at which they can be applied. What you will learn about teaching spelling in this book is not likely to be the way you were taught. It's not likely to be what you are doing in your classroom today, although there are some exceptions. In the remaining chapters of this book, I demonstrate how spelling should be taught and give you practical resources and strategies for teaching it.

3. Change your attitudes about teaching spelling and about spelling's importance for literacy.

That's the goal of this book. Attitudes aren't changed easily or overnight. But give this book a good read. In the following chapters, I guide you through additional discoveries that I believe will lead many educators to challenge their current theories about the place of spelling in the teaching of literacy, and perhaps change their view on the importance of spelling and how to teach it.

How are teaching strategies for young emerging spellers different than those for older skilled spellers, and how does the difference relate to brain scan research?

2

Discovery #2: The Emergence of Spelling Ability and Ability to Spell Words Correctly and Automatically Are Different

Over the years, my synthesis of the spelling research and my work with children convinced me that *learning to spell*, which generally should happen in kindergarten and first grade, is very different from *being a good speller* (that is, spelling words correctly and automatically), which generally evolves in grades two through eight. The two processes are separate phases of literacy development. The first phase—learning to spell—involves learning how to represent words with alphabetic letters as children develop a full understanding of the alphabetic principle. The alphabetic principle and spelling system work differently in the various alphabetic languages. In Italian, for example, it's fairly simple, with one letter for each sound and a few additional combinations. But in English, the alphabetic principle is complex, with a plethora of foreign spellings, myriad spelling combinations, a huge vocabulary, and sometimes arbitrary spelling patterns, such as the seemingly whimsical spelling of compounds: *applesauce, post office,* and *twenty-one,* not *applesauce, postoffice,* and *twenty one.* This complex system of English spelling makes it more difficult to spell than an alphabetic language such as Italian.

Because the English alphabetic principle is complex, children generally need about two years to figure out the English alphabetic principle and use it in the same way that a skilled literate adult uses it. This learning-to-spell process unfolds in stages and results in qualitatively different levels of writing production generally observed in kindergarten

PHASE I. LEARNING TO SPELL				
GENTRY'S LEVELS OF WRITING	EHRI'S PHASES OF WORD LEARNING	GENTRY'S STAGES OF DEVELOPMEN-TAL SPELLING	SPELLING CUR-RICULUM TO BE TAUGHT	EXPECTED COMPETENCY
LEVEL 0 WRITING: No ability to use letters		No ability to use invented spellings	Learning to write one's name; the alphabet song; nursery rhymes and word play; use of techniques leading child to begin to invent Level 1 spellings	Pre-kindergarten
LEVEL 1 WRITING: Use of letters with no matches to sound	PRE-ALPHABETIC WORD READING	PRECOMMUNICA-TIVE SPELLING	Use of techniques leading inventive spellers to Stage 2, plus a few correct spellings gleaned from writing	Beginning to middle of kindergarten
LEVEL 2 WRITING: Use of partial sound–letter matches	PARTIAL ALPHABETIC WORD READING	SEMIPHONETIC SPELLING	Use of techniques leading inventive spellers to Stage 3, plus a few correct spellings gleaned from writing	Middle to end of kindergarten
LEVEL 3 WRITING: Use of one letter for each sound	FULL ALPHABETIC WORD READING	PHONETIC SPELLING	Use of techniques leading inventive spellers to Level 4, plus a few correct spellings gleaned from writing; correct spelling of some high-frequency word families; the first grade corpus	Beginning to middle of first grade
LEVEL 4 WRITING: Use of chunks of phonics patterns	CONSOLIDATED ALPHABETIC WORD READING	TRANSITIONAL SPELLING	Completion of the first grade corpus, including correct spelling of CVC short-vowel patterns and some CVCe long-vowel patterns	Middle to end of first grade

FIGURE 2–1 Learning to Spell

PHASE II. CORRECT AND AUTOMATIC SPELLING		
NEW LEARNING	SPELLING CURRICULUM TO BE TAUGHT	EXPECTED COMPETENCY
The 2nd Grade Corpus	High-frequency 2nd grade words, patterns, and principles	End of 2nd grade
The 3rd Grade Corpus	High-frequency 3rd grade words, patterns, and principles	End of 3rd grade
The 4th Grade Corpus	High-frequency 4th grade words, patterns, and principles	End of 4th grade
The 5th Grade Corpus	High-frequency 5th grade words, patterns, and principles	End of 5th grade
The 6th Grade Corpus	High-frequency 6th grade words, patterns, and principles	End of 6th grade
The 7th Grade Corpus	High-frequency 7th grade words, patterns, and principles	End of 7th grade
The 8th Grade Corpus	High-frequency 8th grade words, patterns, and principles	End of 8th grade

FIGURE 2–1   Continued

through the end of first grade. Ehri, remarkably, has identified the same levels as phases of word learning (1997), highlighting the critical role spelling plays in early reading. The five levels of emergent spelling/writing/reading start with virtually no ability to use letters (Level 0) to using letters without matching them to sounds (Level 1). Development next moves to partial sound–letter matches in a word demonstrating partial phonemic awareness (Level 2), and then to choosing one letter for each sound in the word being spelled, demonstrating full phonemic awareness (Level 3). Finally, children are able to spell, write, or decode words or syllables with chunks of phonics patterns (Level 4). At this last level of Phase I, children spell with letter combinations based on phonics principles, much as you and I do, but they often use the wrong pattern for the word or syllable being spelled. The cumulative result of the developmental process is that children create, almost literally, a "dictionary for words in the brain" for writing, reading, and spelling. Researchers call this dictionary "the lexicon" and have often debated whether the brain actually stores words in spellings or in some more abstract format such as feature analysis. (You will learn at the end of this chapter that there is growing evidence that most highly literate brains store exact neural models of words, including their correct spellings.) The two phases of spelling development are represented in Figure 2–1, with Phase I divided into developmental levels and Phase II divided into instructional levels for learning correct spellings.

Learning to spell, the first phase of spelling acquisition, engages the learner in creating the dictionary for words in the brain. This phase entails learning the system used in a particular alphabetic language to map the detached graphic word to its spoken counterpart—often referred to as "learning the alphabetic principle." Many educators don't realize that for English readers and writers, the process generally takes about two years. At the end of this two-year phase for English spelling, the basic knowledge base for the spelling system (and perhaps the brain circuitry for spelling) is in place. By the end of first grade, seven-year-olds who have reached the last stage in the 0-1-2-3-4 levels of emergent writing know how spelling works. While their word-specific knowledge is inchoate, and while they may produce quite a few incorrect spelling chuncks (such as FRIDE for *fried* or YOUNIGHTED for *united*), their abundant use of phonetically acceptable letter combinations is a signal that the system is up and operational. At this juncture, teachers should look for a major literacy milestone—the child spells a substantial corpus of known spelling and the child invents unknown spelling in chunks of phonics patterns: About two thirds of the child's spelling in a substantial volume of writing is correct, with the child's repertoire of automatic correct spelling reaching upwards of fifty to one hundred or more words. Additionally, the child invents spelling using the basic phonics patterns for combining *consonants* and *vowels* (i.e., CV [*he, we*], CVC [*hop, pet, can*], CVCe [*hope, Pete*], and CVVC [*read, nail*]). For children who can do this, the system is consolidated and operational: They have a lot of word-specific knowledge in their brains, and they have mastered the English alphabetic principle.

Next, a second phase—*spelling correctly and automatically*—must kick in. A lot of word-specific knowledge must be learned *after* Phase I. Many third graders still need to master the consonant doubling/*e*-drop principle—for example, learning how to handle *hopping* and *hoping,* respectively. Fifth grade writers are often found puzzling over whether to use *ei* or *ie,* which may easily be addressed by teaching the "*i* before *e* except after *c* rule." So, from second through sixth or eighth grade, children fine-tune their word-specific knowledge and grow in sophistication using the orthographic system, even as they increase the number of words they can spell accurately and automatically.

Quite different from the early developmental stages of learning to spell, Phase II of spelling advancement concentrates on adding entries to the dictionary in the brain. Once a child fully understands the complexity of the alphabetic principle for English spelling, spells in chunks of letter combinations, and acquires the incipient corpus of fifty or so automatic and correct spellings, the dictionary is established. Now one has several years of word study, reading, and writing to use the system, add correct spelling entries, and grow in ease and accuracy with spelling.

The big job during the second phase of spelling acquisition is adding new, correct spelling entries to the dictionary in the brain. More specifically, children must add correct spellings to the neural models for each word in their brains. According to literacy researcher Linda Allal, "Skill in spelling even more than skill in reading or in mathematics, is primarily a product of school learning" (1997, 129). Good spellers built up large numbers of words and lots of word-specific knowledge in their mental dictionaries. The word-specific knowledge in the poor speller's brain is comparably sparse. Though many educators have not treated it as such, *adding correct spelling entries to the dictionary in the brain* is an important goal for increasing literacy.

Children progress through the second phase of spelling skill acquisition in degrees that are quantifiable according to grade level criteria fitting the notion of instructional levels for spelling (see Figure 2–1) (Henderson 1990; Schlagal 1992). Although the second phase of spelling seems to be more a function of school learning and literacy experience than later developmental stages (Gentry 2000a), there is a quantifiable corpus of high-frequency words and patterns that children might be expected to have mastered at each particular grade level (two through eight). For example, a good speller in second grade might invent (i.e., misspell) up to a third of the words used in writing, while a good speller in third grade invents only 10 percent or less. Likewise, a good speller at grade six has simply acquired more word-specific knowledge than a good speller at grade three, and the percentage of misspelled words in writing is negligible. This child has a much larger reading vocabulary, uses more words, spells more words accurately, and understands more sophisticated spelling principles.

It is relatively easy for researchers to survey large samples of children's writing at each grade level and determine a core curriculum of words, patterns, and spelling principles that students might be expected to acquire at each particular grade level. At each grade level, the teacher observes and assesses each student's word-specific knowledge, and if a student doesn't have the expected word-specific knowledge for a particular grade level, the teacher *teaches* him or her the spelling core curricula principles. This is good spelling instruction. With this instruction, children grow in word-specific knowledge year by year, with reciprocal benefits to writing fluency, reading fluency, and even speaking.

The task of adding more correct spelling entries to the dictionary in the brain is multifaceted. Not all entries are added in the same way; for example, not all spellings are learned one word at a time or by memorizing word lists. Work with a word list, however, when properly implemented, is one efficient way to add entries to the dictionary in the brain. For example, National Spelling Bee champions, a subset of children who are among the world's best spellers, study word lists incessantly, adding words such as *crinoline, succedaneum,* and *prospicience,* displaying phe-nomenal fervor for explicit word study (Blitz 2003).

There are a number of ways other than studying words in lists to add entries to the dictionary in the brain. Words may be added by remembering certain spelling patterns, a process enhanced by word sorting, or by remembering analogies to known spellings. Accurate spelling of some words is remembered when the speller applies a few good spelling rules—the "*i* before *e* except after *c*" rule comes to mind. Words may be remembered by using mnemonic devices such as "There is *a rat* in sepARATe." I will concede that some words are probably remembered by noticing spellings in reading, but I believe the effectiveness of this method is way down on the list. In addition to studying word lists, there is evidence that spelling accuracy is enhanced by getting in the habit of correcting one's spelling in writing, collecting the misspelled words, and studying them explicitly (Allal 1997; Gentry 2002; Graham 1983; Peters 1985).

A few words might be remembered in unusual ways. For example, I suspect a few spellings are remembered kinesthetically by remembering the movement required in spelling a word on a keyboard or a touch pad, but probably not by remembering the sweep of a pen or cheerleading letter formations, such as the hand motions used with the pop tune "YMCA." Spelling for writing and typing is interesting. I can see a word or think a word and type it or write it automatically without repeating the letters. This may be additional evidence that *spellings* may be stored in the brain and retrieved automatically. It would be interesting to see what additional brain circuitry is functioning when the spelling is typed automatically versus spelled out loud at a spelling bee.

In proficient spellers, the dictionary in the brain seems to operate somewhat like a computer spelling checker that expert spellers use very effectively. They can tell whether a particular spelling "looks right," probably by activating certain areas of the brain that process spellings visually. By the end of third grade or by fourth grade, good spellers generally have enough word-specific knowledge that they begin to use this strategy to their advantage.

Recent brain scan research provides compelling evidence for the two phases of spelling development described previously: Phase I, the emergence of spelling ability, and a second phase, beginning around second grade for most students, for learning the word-specific knowledge required to spell words automatically. Magnetic resonance scans of the brain may guide us to a clearer understanding of these phases; of how spelling, reading, and writing are connected; and of clinically significant aspects of spelling impairment.

In a series of *functional* magnetic resonance imagery (fMRI) studies conducted by a Yale neuroscientist and her colleagues, Sally Shaywitz

(2003) reports that the studies reveal how learning to read and skilled reading are different: "Imaging studies have identified at least two neural pathways for reading: one for beginning reading, for slowly sounding out words, and another that is a speedier pathway for skilled reading" (78). I believe that these two neural pathways for reading are directly related to the two phases of spelling. Shaywitz goes on to report, "Beginning readers must first analyze a word; skilled readers identify a word instantaneously" (79). This finding matches the two phases of spelling/reading/writing development. The descriptions of Ehri's early phases of word learning in "Learning to Read and Learning to Spell Are One and the Same, Almost" (1997) and Gentry's descriptions of early developmental stages of invented spelling and writing seem to be corroborated by the Shaywitz brain scan work. Ehri's phases of word learning, Gentry's stages of spelling, and Shaywitz's description of two neural pathways all describe two phases of spelling/reading/writing with an early phase for learning the processes, which essentially entails "breaking the code," and a second phase, which Shaywitz describes as a later speedier pathway, when word analysis becomes automatic (78). In my interpretation of the Shaywitz work, the first phase unfolds as the emerging speller/writer/reader learns to convert alphabetic characters to a linguistic code, a process in which written words are decoded or encoded into the phonemes of the speech stream. This breaking-the-code phase unfolds in four previously described stages:

Level 1: Use of letters without matching them to sounds

Level 2: Sound–letter matches in a word, demonstrating partial phonemic awareness

Level 3: Choosing one letter for each sound in the word being spelled, demonstrating full phonemic awareness

Level 4: Spelling each word with chunks of spelling patterns

Keep in mind that a very young child who can neither read, write, nor spell already has a neural circuitry in place for smooth and seamless spoken language and uses phonemes, words, phrases, and sentences unconsciously. Learning spoken language is natural and instinctive for the child. His or her brain is wired up with an innate speaking ability found in every normal human brain, though not in the brain of a cat, an iguana, or a parrot. Preconscious and automatic ability to speak is easily acquired by most children during the first few years of life, regardless of the spoken-language culture into which the child is born. But around the age of five or six, the child enters kindergarten and is confronted with what can be a formidable task. The English-speaking child must learn to write and read spellings. Writing and reading is harder to learn than speaking. Unlike the brain's innate capacity for learning to speak, there is no circuitry for automatic writing and reading. Writing and reading has to be taught. The reader must reconstruct the sound of the language by looking at print and mapping the print onto the already existing spoken language circuitry (Shaywitz 2003). The success of this endeavor hinges on how well the child is able to become aware of and manipulate the phonology of language. Learning to write and read is intimately tied to the process of bringing the segmental nature of speech into consciousness. As the child passes through the developmental stages listed above, he or she becomes increasingly aware of the segmental nature of spoken language and grows in sophistication in how he or she uses the basic elements of written language—first using letters, then letters for sounds, then one letter for every sound in a word, and finally chunks of phonics patterns or letter combinations. According to Shaywitz, the spellings of printed language are transformed in the brain to speech and meaning as the neural circuitry already in place for speech accepts the language that is translated from print. Print is a code of spellings. Once the code is broken, the brain turns the *spellings* of printed language into flowing speech as the reading circuitry maps the spellings into meaningful speech.

I believe that emerging readers who invent spellings are literally establishing a neural circuitry. Although I am not a neuroscientist, I predict that fMRIs could possibly show brain circuitry development in lockstep with the reported stages of early spelling and writing. Given the Ehri work, which demonstrates that phases of word learning for reading and stages of developmental spelling are the same, and given the Shaywitz description of the revelation of two phases—first, learning to read, and later, automatic skilled reading—there appears to be a neurological basis for developmental stages of spelling and writing. The brain scan studies corroborate the developmental spelling theory.

In her book, *Overcoming Dyslexia*, Shaywitz purports that the pathways in the brain for reading, and even the function of specific neural systems, have been identified. She reports that reading ability resides within the language system in the brain and that scientists have been able to pinpoint the precise locations for three basic components. Some critiques of Shaywitz's work and of studies funded by the National Institute of Child Health and Human Development (NICHD) consider the work to be "bad science that hurts children," believing it to be part of a conspiracy to promote skills-emphasis instruction (Coles 2000). There are dissenting views even among those who do functional imagery studies and reports that "exact correlation between cortical language areas and subcomponents of the linguistic system has not been established" (Embick et al. 2000). My own view is that direct evidence of "the existence of distinct modules for our knowledge of language" (Embick et al. 2000, 6150) is compelling work, and I don't find it unreasonably complex or mystifying. In my opinion, there will never be a time when "scientists can confidently design a classroom curriculum based completely on neuro-science," as some might suggest (Hotz 1998). I do believe we educators should take this work seriously and consider it in light of our professional knowledge, educational philosophy, the education research base, and our classroom experience.

Visualize the left half of your brain. Now divide the left half of your brain into three areas: (1) the front, (2) the left side just above and slightly behind the ear, and (3) a third area lower and to the back of the head. According to Shaywitz, these areas play the major roles for reading in normally functioning readers. These three major neural pathways for phonological analysis work together much like an orchestra, according to Shaywitz, who reports that the first two areas are slow and analytic and most important during the first phase of literacy development as children *become* readers/writers/spellers.

Shaywitz says that brain scans have revealed that the area in the front of the brain (the left inferior frontal gyrus in Broca's area) helps the emerging reader vocalize and subvocalize words by analyzing phonemes. In lay terms, this part of the brain has been called "the phoneme processor" (Gorman 2003, 56). Shaywitz describes this area as "the functional part of the brain where sounds of language are put together to form words" (2003, 40).

The area above and slightly behind the ear (the left parietotemporal system) is also important for beginning readers. As described by Shaywitz, "Slow and analytic, its functions seems to be in the early stages of learning to read, that is, in initially analyzing a word, pulling it apart, and linking its letters to their sounds" (2003, 79). This area is the neural site for sounding out words.

Shaywitz says the third area behind the ear and in the back of the brain is the one used by skilled readers to process reading automatically (left occipitotemporal area). (The location of this area may explain a biological basis for the high occurrence of early ear infections in children who later experience reading difficulty.) She calls this area "the express pathway to reading" (79). Once the speller/reader/writer enters Phase II, just as they are becoming skilled second grade–level readers, they are able to access this area to identify words instantaneously with no analysis. This area "reacts to the whole word as a pattern" and identifies the word automatically on sight. Educators have long recognized automatic sight word recognition of 100 or more words as a watershed event in the development of a reader. According to Shaywitz, when this area is activated in a skilled reader, the child is able to form "an exact neural model of a specific word." While not being specific, she indicates that there are certain brain regions dedicated to processing the visual features of print and points to this third occipitotemporal area as the place where the brain stores relevant information about words—not only the meaning and how it sounds, *but also the spelling!* Of course, Shaywitz doesn't claim the correct spelling just automatically appears in the neural model. For most children, spelling has to be taught.

Shaywitz's description of an automatic phase and her assertion that brain scan studies indicate that normal brains store not only word meanings, but also their spellings, is a good fit with my long-held theory that the normally functioning brain can see words (spellings) in the mind's eye and that one in five of us who are severely spelling disabled simply cannot see them!

Implications

Implications from the discovery that the emergence of spelling and correct and automatic spelling are different fall into two categories. The first set of implications relates to the emergence phase of spelling/writing/reading. The last implication relates to Phase II.

1. Kindergarteners and first graders should invent spellings and write frequently because writing helps them develop underlying knowledge sources for reading, such as knowledge of sounds, letters, phonological awareness, phonemic awareness, and, eventually, recognition and use of chunks of phonics patterns. Teachers should highlight the reciprocal relationship of spelling, writing, and reading instruction.

2. Pay attention to developmental levels of spelling in kindergarten and first grade writing. The four stages are easy to recognize and monitor simply by classifying the child as meeting the specifications of a particular writing level when up to one-half of his or her invented spelling in voluminous writing fits the description of a particular level (Gentry 1982) (see Figure 2–1). Use informal assessments such as the Monster Test (Gentry 1982) to further track development in Phase I. (See Appendix A.)

3. Differentiate instruction during Phase I based on *levels of writing.* Because students in a kindergarten or first grade classroom are likely to be functioning at various writing levels, match the type and timing of instruction with the specific needs of the writer to help him or her move to the next higher writing level. This differentiated instruction is a key to the successful teaching of literacy. (Specific teaching strategies appropriate at each writing level are highlighted in Chapter 3.)

4. Provide early intervention during Phase I for students who are not meeting expected levels of writing achievement. Use strategic teaching to help students move to the next highest level. Informally monitor the degree to which students are beginning to develop the ability to spell some words automatically, expecting a gradual increase in the number of correctly spelled words in voluminous writing during

Phase I. (Levels should approach 66 percent correct spelling by the end of Writing Level 4.) Keeping personal spelling journals of "Words I Can Spell," collected from children's writing, might enhance such monitoring. Conduct informal spelling checks of high-frequency spelling words and patterns and teach a corpus of first grade–level spelling words and phonics patterns as part of the grade one curriculum.

5. Provide explicit spelling instruction during Phase II for increasing writing and reading fluency. Assess second through eighth grade spellers to determine if their word-specific knowledge meets expectations for a corpus of high-frequency words and patterns at each grade level. Teach words and patterns students do not know. (Chapters 3 and 4 survey teaching methods, and Chapter 5 demonstrates a framework to teach spelling in grades two through eight.)

How can you lead the emerging writer/reader/speller to higher levels of development?

3

Discovery #3: You Can Recognize Five Levels of Emergent Writing, Match Your Teaching Strategies to the Child's Level, and Greatly Improve the Quality of Your Literacy Instruction

Sometimes we know more than we think we do. We may have an almost fully developed understanding of a complex process like how to cast exactly where the bass will strike, how to deal with grief after experiencing the tragic loss of a brother, or how best to handle the simultaneous joys and exigencies of caring for an elderly and failing parent, then something unexpected happens to shed new light on the old problem. Often another person shows a new way to look at it or offers some new insight, and (ah-Ha!) we see the complex issue more clearly than ever before—so clearly in light of this new discovery that we may never go back to the old way of looking at the issue. That happened to me as a spelling researcher, and I hope it will happen to you by reading this chapter. While many readers of this book already have a deep and full understanding of teaching beginning reading, I hope to demonstrate how adding the spelling–writing connection to teaching emergent literacy not only clarifies a spelling pathway each child must negotiate in taking the first steps to literacy development, but also charts the focus of your teaching by allowing you to facilitate the writer/reader/speller's move to higher levels of independence. Understanding the spelling–writing pathway may change not only how you view emergent readers, but also how you teach them.

The "ah-Ha" phenomenon happened for me when I read a research paper entitled "Scaffolding Emergent Writing in the Zone of Proximal

Development" by two outstanding researchers in early childhood education, Elena Bodrova and Deborah Leong (1998). I was reading along in
the article and came to a section in which Bodrova and Leong described
"Gentry's Scale of Writing" (11). "Gentry's scale was chosen because it
had the clearest and most detailed definitions of the characteristics of
each level," they reported (12). But what was phenomenal to me was that
they had seen the spelling scale that I had developed as clearly more than
developmental spelling. It was, in fact, "a writing scale!" Bodrova and
Leong demonstrated the scope of its use beyond tracking stages of
invented spelling by using it to show how children who are emerging in
literacy changed their conception of the alphabetic principle as they
emerge as writers. My "ah-Ha" moment was that the scale and developmental spelling stages were much more important for overall literacy
development than I had ever realized. More recently, researchers in Por-
tugal, Silva and Alves-Martins, describe the same scale as "stages in the
development of writing" in their study tracking preschool children who
are developing conceptualizations of phonological skills and writing,
giving the scale legitimacy across cultures (2002, 470). And while the
scale has been used for years by thousands of teachers in the form of "The
Monster Test" (see Appendix A) and by educators such as Eilene Feldgus
and Isabell Cardonick to track emergent writing development in their
framework for teaching emergent writing in the kindergarten classroom
(1999), it never really occurred to me how powerful the scale is for chart-
ing not only spelling, but also development of writing and reading as literacy unfolds. *I believe it to be one of the most powerful tools in existence for
measuring important aspects of early literacy development.*

In "Scaffolding Emergent Writing in the Zone of Proximal Development," Bodrova and Leong bring to bear their very rich grounding in the
Vygotskian tradition, including specific teaching techniques that I have
included as I match teaching techniques with writing levels in this chapter. For me, their work crystallized with Ehri's (1997) notion that reading
phases of word learning dovetail with spelling stages and also with Juel's
(1994) idea regarding the importance of the type and timing of early literacy instruction. While Marie Clay's (1993) brilliant work had enlight-
ened us to certain aspects of emergent literacy, this new work adds the
writing–spelling connection that, up until now, has been misunderstood
or totally missing.

The problem with teaching reading is that reading is complex and
what the child knows or does not know is often hidden. The teacher cannot *see* what the reader knows. Of course, with techniques such as miscue
analysis, the teacher can make analyses of how the child uses various language systems—phonological, syntactic, semantic—but wouldn't a direct
measure of what the emergent reader knows or does not know be useful?
That's where analysis of developmental spelling comes in. With writing,

the teacher *can see* what the student knows and does not know quite explicitly. The way the child spells is like a visible footprint of how he or she thinks the code works. Does the child know that letters represent sounds? Is the child deciphering at a complex level of phonics patterns or is the processing at a level of paying attention to prominent letters (usually beginning and ending letters) based on partial letter cues or is it some even lower level of processing? If the level of processing is complex, what particular phonics patterns does this child know or not know? Once the teacher sees what the child knows, the teacher knows what to teach.

In this chapter we begin with an overview of the five levels of writing by inspecting samples of writing that show what children do at each level. We look at a set of teaching techniques that are particularly well suited for children at the emergent levels of writing/reading/spelling. We then revisit the same samples from a particular perspective: *What strategies work best to move the child to the next highest level?* The type of instruction recommended at each level fits with a particular phase or stage of development. Sections of this chapter are reprinted, with permission, from my article, "Instructional Techniques for Emerging Writers and Special Needs Students at Kindergarten and Grade 1 Levels" (in press).

The Writing Scale

The Gentry Writing Scale, identifies levels of emergent writing by marking progress from one level to the next in terms of symbol versus letter formation, completeness of phonemic representation, qualitative differences in invented spelling based on sophistication of letter–sound correspondence, and representation of the alphabetic principle. The scale measures qualitative changes in how the writer conceptualizes and uses the alphabetic system as a tool for writing. It represents five stages in the child's knowledge of how the system of print works and shows how the child applies this knowledge in writing. The teacher uses this information to help determine the type and timing of appropriate instruction (Juel 1994) and to help the writer move to the next higher level than the level where he or she functions independently.

Five stages are shown, beginning with approximations (i.e., no letters) and moving to Level 1—writing in letters with no matches to sound; to Level 2—writing with partial representations of sounds in words; to Level 3—writing with full phonetic representation connecting each sound in a word to a printed letter; to Level 4—writing with more sophisticated representations, consolidating phonics knowledge, marking vowels, and spelling in chunks of letter patterns. A child is considered to be in a particular stage when more than half of his or her invented spellings fit the stage criteria (Gentry 2000a). The terms *pre-alphabetic, partial alphabetic, full alphabetic,* and *consolidated alphabetic,* borrowed from Ehri

(1997), are good descriptors of the writer's changing conception of how the alphabet system works. The scale is not exhaustive; for example, it is not used to illustrate writing issues such as communicating meaning, genre, or types of writing, such as narrative versus persuasive, descriptive, or expository writing. Other considerations, such as standards of volume and quantitative changes in emergent writing over time, are discussed in this chapter in the section on framing writing.

In the initial Level 0, non-alphabetic writing, the writer may scribble or approximate letter forms but not use true alphabetic letters. Spellings are not yet invented. The child doesn't know the system for how print works.

The next stage is the first stage at which the writer uses the alphabet. Level 1 is a pre-alphabetic stage. Before the writer understands the alphabetic principle, he or she may write with letters that appear to be random because there is no letter–sound correspondence. At this level the writer uses letters but has not grasped that there is a relation between letters and sounds.

Level 2 is a partial alphabetic stage. Letters *are* used to represent sounds, but due to limitations in the writer's knowledge about letters and sounds and how they work together, the writer is able to provide only partial alphabetic representations. The child is beginning to figure out how the system of print works. Typically these partial alphabetic spellings represent prominent sounds in words and generally consist of consonants such as BT for *boat*. Sometimes long vowels and other letter name spellings are employed at Level 2, such as A followed by T for *eighty*. Level 2 writers may sprinkle their invented spelling with a few memorized spellings, rendering readable messages such as MY MR BT for *my motor boat*.

Level 3 is full alphabetic writing. In contrast to the Level 2 partial representation of sounds, virtually all the phonemes in a word are represented by matching a sound to a letter. Thus, MOTR BOT replaces the earlier MT BT for *motor boat*, with the *R* in the last syllable of *motor* carrying the vowel sound. Level 3 spelling may be accompanied by more learned spellings, as this is a middle first grade benchmark and children typically have learned to spell quite a few sight words correctly by the time they write at Level 3.

Level 4 is a consolidated alphabetic stage. The writer goes beyond strategies for spelling each sound with a single letter and begins to spell syllables and one-syllable words in chunks of letter patterns, such as CVCe and CVVC. Here the writer is able to apply knowledge of basic phonics patterns in writing and uses known spellings to cope with novel words such as YOUNIGHTED for *united*. At this level, the writer tends to spell short vowels conventionally and up to two-thirds of words used correctly. He or she has consolidated the basic underlying knowledge systems for writing (and reading), including an understanding of basic phonics patterns and a full grasp of how the system of print works.

The Gentry Writing Scale may be used to establish a minimal qualitative competency standard or benchmark to help teachers measure an individual's growth against what might be expected over time (Gentry 2000a, 2000b). The minimal expected progress in writing development is as follows:

Level 0—Beginning kindergarten

Level 1—Middle of kindergarten

Level 2—End of kindergarten

Level 3—Middle of first grade

Level 4—End of first grade

The writing scale also helps teachers track the development of the child's changing conceptualization of how the alphabet system works. Writers can function as writers even when they are unsophisticated in their understanding of how the alphabet system works (i.e., Stages 1 and 2). The scale pays homage to a basic principle of language learning that function precedes perfect form.

Now let's look at writing samples that represent each level. Antonio, whose writing appears in Figure 3–1, is a Level 0 non-alphabetic writer. He cannot yet use letters, and he doesn't know how to write his name. He is functioning at a symbol representation stage, using wavy writing or, in some cases, loopy writing. Writing at this stage is represented by marks, scribbles, and pictures. No discernable letters are present. The child does not grasp how the system works. It is important to note that spellings are not yet invented at the non-alphabetic writing level. A minimal competency for Level 0 is expected by the beginning of kindergarten.

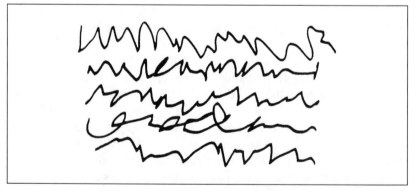

FIGURE 3–1   Level 0—Non-Alphabetic Writing (Antonio)

FIGURE 3-2   Level 1—Pre-Alphabetic Writing (Leslie)

Leslie, whose writing appears in Figure 3-2, is a Level 1 pre-alphabetic writer. She begins to show some control of letters, but her letters do not represent sounds. Neither Leslie nor others can read this message out of context or after a lapse in time. At this level, Leslie does not know how the system of print works. She is a pre-communicative speller; that is, her messages are spelled in strings of letters, but there are no sound–letter matches. Letters may appear to be strung randomly. Sometimes, spacing may not occur between words at this level. Phonemic awareness is not evident. Minimal competency for Level 1 is expected by mid kindergarten.

Michael is a Level 2 partial alphabetic writer. His writing, which appears in Figure 3-3, does not provide complete phonemic representation. Writers at this level often abbreviate, using a few letter–sound matches mixed with random letters. Directionality generally is present. A few correct spellings may appear in the message. The writer begins to connect the sounds within a word to letters, which is the hallmark of their semi-phonetic spelling. Prominent sounds are spelled with letter–sound matches. Some of the sounds in the invented words are not represented, though some phonemic awareness is evident. Minimal competency for Level 2 is expected by the end of kindergarten.

Julie, who wrote "The Three Little Pigs" in Figure 3-4, is a Level 3 full alphabetic writer. Notice in her spellings of WOD'S for *woods*, FRST for *first*, LITL for *little*, BUNDL for *bundle*, and UV for *of*, that all phonemes in each of these words are spelled with a single letter. At Level 3 the writer provides

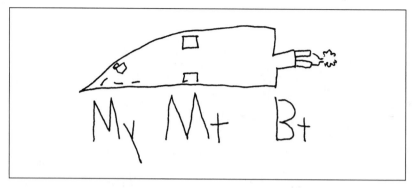

FIGURE 3–3 Level 2—Partial Alphabetic Writing (Michael)

full phonemic representation in novel words, using a letter for each sound. The writing is easy to read phonetically, but writing such as ATE for *eighty* doesn't always look like English spelling. More words are spelled

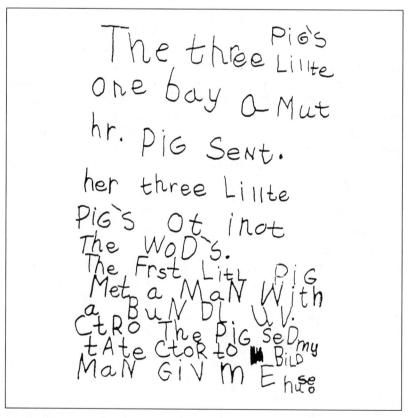

FIGURE 3–4 Level 3—Full Alphabetic Writing (Julie)

Good THING to Eat

I like STRALBARES and i like ORRANGE.
I like tomato SUPE and I like PECHIS.
I like apples and I like BROCLE.
I like COLEFLAWORE TO, you know.
I like corn and I like green BENES.
I like FRIDE CEKEN and I like BARBO Q CEKEN TO.
But most of all I like HO MAED SPOGATE.
THOSS things are good for you.
That's why I put them down.

FIGURE 3–5   Level 4—Consolidated Alphabetic Writing (Tameka)

correctly than at previous levels. Level 3 writers are phonetic spellers (sometimes called letter–name), and they provide a letter for each sound in a novel word. Virtually all of the sounds in the word are represented, including vowels. Full phonemic awareness is evident at Level 3; however, medial short vowels are often misspelled. Minimal competency is expected by the middle of first grade.

Tameka, who wrote "Good Thing to Eat" in Figure 3–5 at the beginning of her second grade year, is a Level 4 consolidated alphabetic writer. Notice the extent of her word-specific knowledge for correct spellings: She spells many first grade–level words correctly. At this level, the writer has consolidated his or her knowledge of how the alphabet system works and generally about two-thirds of the words are spelled correctly. The writer applies more sophisticated phonics patterns in writing, moving beyond one-to-one sound–letter matches. Level 4 writers are transitional spellers (sometimes called within-word pattern): Novel words are invented in syllables, and chunks of spelling patterns and short vowels are spelled conventionally. One-syllable long-vowel patterns such as CVCe and CVVC are recognized and used, though word-specific knowledge for correct spellings may be incomplete (e.g., MENE or MEEN for *mean*). Minimal competency for Level 4 is expected by the end of first grade.

Before we go back and discuss what teaching strategies to use for each level, here's an overview of some of the important teaching strategies we will highlight.

Techniques Defined

In exemplary kindergarten writing experiences, I have observed seven techniques that may be used effectively to support emergent writing and guide very young children to independence and development as writers: creating a writing block, teaching in the zone of proximal development, use of private speech, use of scaffolded writing, materialization, adult underwriting, and story framing. As director of a university reading center for ten years, I have also observed many struggling learners or learning disabled writers who functioned at kindergarten and first grade—levels benefit from the same instructional strategies. I recommend more research to validate the efficacy of their use with these special populations.

Creating a Writing Block

Writing may be the most important part of the kindergarten curriculum. It enhances children's letter knowledge and phonemic awareness skills and leads to success with reading in first grade (Juel 1994; Snow, Burns, and Griffin 1998). Because writing takes time, all kindergarten classrooms should provide a block of time for children to write and to receive instruction in writing. The models I observe that seem most effective allow for at least forty-five minutes a day of kindergarten writing and include whole class minilessons, time for independent writing, and time for sharing. Student choice for topics and drawing pictures of the concept being written about are hallmarks for prewriting in kindergarten. All students write independently every day, or approximate writing every day, beginning at whatever level they are capable and receiving developmentally appropriate instruction that helps them move to the next level. Students often move through two or three levels of development during the kindergarten year; consequently, teachers always have students who require a range of different instructional needs and responses. Teachers provide writing instruction during the writing block by modeling in whole class groups and by providing a great deal of differentiated instruction in small groups and in one-on-one roving conferences (Feldgus and Cardonick 1999). A framework for the writing block is presented in Figure 3–6. The times that are recommended for each segment are flexible, depending on the nature of the activity and the particular needs of the group.

Teaching in the Zone of Proximal Development

Teaching in the zone of proximal development, a Vygotskian concept, resonates with developmentally appropriate instruction or teaching in a child's range of capability (Vygotsky 1978). This concept suggests that there is a tie between instruction and a child's development and that the best instruction moves children to higher levels of independence (Bodrova and Leong 1998). In the context of teaching writing in kindergarten and first grade, developmental levels of writing may be identified,

---

Teaching Block (15 minutes)

Activities   Minilessons/Teacher modeling/Shared and
                                       interactive writing

Writing Block (20 to 25 minutes)

Activities   Individual student writing or planning for
                                       writing/Teacher roving/Individual and small
                                       group work

Sharing Block (5 to 10 minutes)

Activities   Student sharing/Discussions/Planning for
                                       writing

FIGURE 3–6   A Framework for Kindergarten Writing Workshop

allowing the teacher to model and scaffold the writer's move to the next highest level of writing.

Use of Private Speech

Private speech is self-directed regulatory speech used by the learner to give himself or herself auditory directions to support the development of new mental actions (Galperin 1969, 1992; Bodrova and Leong 1998, 5). This temporary support mechanism is dropped once the process is internalized. Private speech may often be observed among emergent writers; for example, a child might repeat out loud the words he or she intends to write: "I went to the Harry Potter movie." Another example of private speech is when the child rehearses out loud a known spelling such as *the*, by repeating *t-h-e* out loud.

Use of Scaffolded Writing

Bodrova and Leong attribute the term *scaffolding* to Bruner (Wood, Bruner, and Ross 1976) and indicate that it is used "to specify the types of assistance that make it possible for learners to function at higher levels . . ." (1998, 4–5). The scaffold provides the support necessary for the learner to complete a task at the next higher level than the current independent level of functioning. Once the learner can complete the task at the next higher level independently, the scaffolding that led to that level is no longer needed. This echoes the Vygotskian concept that what the learner can do today with assistance he or she can do tomorrow independently (Vygotsky 1987).

Bodrova and Leong (1998) outline five steps in their scaffolded writing technique for beginners.

1. The child chooses a topic and draws a picture. He/she selects words that go with the picture or tell a related story.

2. The child draws lines for each word in the message with a highlighter. Longer stories may be planned in sections with the child writing one sentence or phrase at the time. Often lines are longer for "longer words" containing more phonemes. For example, "elephant" gets a longer line than "bee."

3. The child uses *private speech:* He/she rehearses the sentence to be written matching each highlighted line with a word in the sentence by saying the sentence out loud and pointing to the line where the word will be written.

4. The child says the word that corresponds to a line in the message and then writes it on the line at whatever level he/she can (i.e., non-alphabetic, Level 1, Level 2, Level 3, or Level 4). Sometimes the child needs to go back and rehearse the message to figure out what word comes next in the sequence.

5. If the message has more than one sentence or phrase, the child highlights and writes one sentence or phrase at a time. Eventually the child will discontinue the use of the highlighted line and write independently without the scaffold. (9–10)

Bodrova and Leong's Scaffolded Writing enables a writer to work independently. In a broader interpretation of scaffolding writing, the teacher may provide an audible and visual scaffold by talking the child through the writing of a piece word by word, providing whatever support the child might need that will eventually lead to independence.

Materialization

Materialization, a Vygotskian concept, involves using a tangible object or a physical action to represent a mental construct (Galperin 1969; Bodrova and Leong 1998). Examples of materialization used effectively with emergent writers include the following:

Letter Boxes. Letter boxes (also called sound boxes or Elkonin boxes) may be used to materialize a writer's awareness of the constituent sounds in a word. When using letter boxes, the child sees a physical object—the box—and experiences the physical action of moving a marker into the box as the phoneme is articulated. Seeing the box and moving the marker "stand for" the sequence of sounds articulated when the word is pronounced. Letter boxes may also materialize the spelling of each phoneme in a word, allowing the emergent writer to spell each sound by placing a letter in the box that stands for the sound being spelled. The process continues box by box until the constituent sounds in the word are spelled (Clay 1993). Because sounds can't be seen, letter boxes effectively add a visual and kinesthetic component to the abstract task of analyzing sounds in words in temporal order.

A Level 2 partial alphabetic writer may be able to get prominent sounds independently, such as the beginning and ending sounds of a word. The letter box can be used to materialize the medial sound, enabling the child to provide the full alphabetic representation. In this example, the letter box is used to materialize the child's movement from a Stage 2 partial alphabetic spelling to a Stage 3 full alphabetic developmentally more advanced representation.

Hand Spelling. Hand spelling is a technique I devised to materialize onsets and rimes. It is well established that children benefit from work with onsets and rimes because these units of sound are psychologically perceptible (Goswami 1996). The onset is defined as whatever sound comes before the vowel. The rime is the chunk that starts with the vowel and completes the word. If you pronounce the sounds in the following words, based on the indicated divisions, you have divided them into onsets and rimes:

Word	Onset	Rime
bat	/ b /	/-at /
hat	/ h /	/-at /
hit	/ h /	/-it /
splat	/ spl /	/-at /
dish	/ d /	/-ish /
bean	/ b /	/-ean /

Traditionally, teachers focused on word families, which, in essence, highlighted the use of onsets and rimes; therefore, in addition to being research based, the technique is supported by conventional wisdom.

Hand spelling is depicted in Figure 3–7 and works as follows: Pronounce the word and represent it with a balled-up fist. Next, pronounce the onset and hold up the thumb. Then pronounce the rime and extend the rest of the hand into the handshake position. Now pronounce the whole word again, returning to the fist position (symbolically pulling the onset and rime back into the whole word). This activity increases phonological awareness by calling to the child's attention—and materializing—the beginning sounds or blends and the phonics chunks that follow the onset. Once children can do hand spelling to designate onsets and rimes, it's very easy for them to move to finger spelling to represent each phoneme in a word.

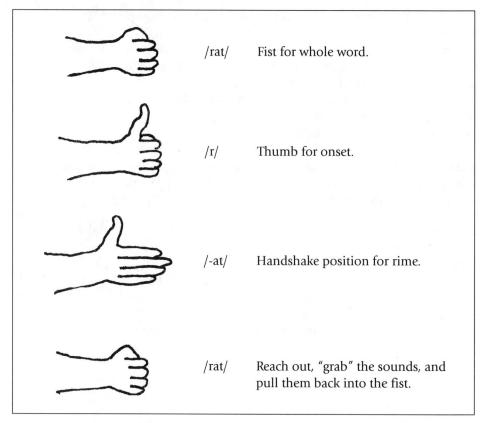

/rat/   Fist for whole word.

/r/   Thumb for onset.

/-at/   Handshake position for rime.

/rat/   Reach out, "grab" the sounds, and
           pull them back into the fist.

FIGURE 3–7   Hand Spelling

Finger Spelling. Finger spelling is an example of physically matching a sound to be spelled with finger movement, followed by the physical movement of "grabbing the word," which stands for collecting the constituent sounds and making them into "a word." It's a physical action that equates with "sounding out a word" to be spelled.

Stretching out the Sounds in a Word. This technique may be materialized by stretching out stretchable fabric as phonemes in a word are exaggerated and pronounced slowly so that the phonemes become more easily recognized as separate entities, and then, with the release of the stretched fabric, the word is pronounced normally to both visually and audibly show how it's the same word as the stretched-out word. The tangible object (the fabric) stands for a word in its a stretched-out state and then in its normal state.

Materialization takes advantage of the social context of learning. Bodrova and Leong report that a number of researchers have demonstrated that students benefit not only from the special instructional techniques associated with materialization, but also from the social interaction with the teacher or tutor (Bodrova and Leong 1998; Elkonin 1963; Galperin 1992).

Adult Underwriting

Adult underwriting is a technique introduced to me by Eileen Feldgus and Isabell Cardonick and also reported in their book, *Kid Writing* (1999). Once the child at Levels 0 to 2 has completed a short written piece—often a few words or phrases to label a picture—the teacher or tutor models the "adult writing" of the same message by writing under the child's production at the bottom of the paper with the same words per line and same sequence of lines as the child produced (see Figure 6–2). For Level 0 up to Level 2, adult underwriting not only gives the teacher the opportunity to model letter formation, concept of word, conventional spelling, and other features of writing, but also gives the teacher a model from which to praise the child's "kid writing" and point out what adult features are already showing up in the child's writing.

Note that the correct spelling is provided so that the child can *read* it, not as a correction of the child's spelling. The most important aspect of adult underwriting for writers at Levels 0 to 2 is that writing is collected in the child's Kindergarten Writing Journal, and the adult underwriting becomes wonderful material for *reading*. The child revisits his or her Kindergarten Writing Journal daily during independent reading to practice rereading and sharing with others the labels or stories he or she has been writing. In actuality, this variation of the traditional language experience approach (Stauffer 1969, 1980) brings a direct reading connection to the writing and spelling program.

It is interesting to note that adult underwriting in the Kindergarten Writing Journal often matches the characteristics of early leveled texts (i.e., Levels 1 and 2 or A and B) that Level 0 to 2 writers often are using in guided reading. That is, the adult underwriting of the child's written productions often has three to five words on a page; has a clear print-to-illustration match; often reflects a concept with which the writer or reader is familiar, making it easy to read; and often contains a repeated sentence stem. This fact further enhances the value of using adult underwriting as important content for the child's *reading* program.

Story Framing

As noted earlier, the Gentry Writing Scale is not exhaustive. Story framing provides a complementary quantitative vehicle for leading emerging writers to higher levels of independence simultaneous with the qualitative developmental aspects of the Gentry Writing Scale. With story framing, the teacher tries to increase the volume of writing. One way to do this

First	Then	Next	Last

FIGURE 3–8   Story Framing

is to match the expected volume to the level of the child's capability. I see two major ways to use story framing: (1) consolidate elaborate oral stories and (2) expand written stories that are not elaborate enough.

In situations in which the child's verbal account of a story to be written may be far more elaborate than his or her capacity for writing, story framing enables the child to write a shorter version of the experience. For example, in Figure 3–2, Leslie's elaborate account of a trip to the meadow and being surrounded by "a flock of butterflies" may be scaffolded using her own words: "a flock of butterflies." At Level 1, she is not yet sophisticated enough as a writer to write the elaborate oral account.

A second use of story framing is to increase the volume of writing. The Story Frame in Figure 3–8 was used to increase three- or four-line

Level 1	**One-Word Story Frames** Labeling Pictures
Level 2	**Phrase Stories Frames** Initially two words such as "My _____" progressing over several weeks to three or four words: "My _____ _____. As in "My motor boat" or "I like _____ _____." As in "I like apple juice."
Level 3	**Sentence Story Frames** "A _____ is a _____ for me."
Level 4	**Line Story Frames** Line stories start at three lines and grow to about six lines.
Level 5	**Elaborate Story Frames** These have components such as Beginning, Middle, Ending; or Day 1, Day 2, Day 3, Day 4; or First, Then, Next, Last.

- Teacher models writing using the story frame that best suits the level of the child.
- Teacher nudges the child to the next level when the child seems ready.
- Teacher uses shared and interactive writing to model various story frames to the whole class.

FIGURE 3–9   Quantitative Levels of Emergent Writing

stories to full-page or multiple-page stories (see also Figure 6–4). The quantitative levels of emergent writing I have observed in kindergarten and first grade fit the progression in Figure 3–9.

I have not observed a direct match between the quantitative levels shown in Figure 3–9 and the qualitative levels of writing in the Gentry Writing Scale. Sometimes low-level writers, even as low as Level 1 on the Gentry Writing Scale, go through spurts or phases in which they produce pages and pages of writing. Generally, however, One-Word Stories, Phrase Stories, Sentence Stories, and Line Stories are the story frames most often used by Level 0 to 2 writers.

It's important to employ instructional techniques best suited for moving writers to the next level of development. Begin with Level 0 writers by teaching them to write their names. Focus on teaching letter recognition and production throughout Levels 0 to 2. Once children can write their names they can move directly to using letters to fill in the highlighted lines of writing scaffolds, which are useful up through Level 3. Use materialization techniques such as clapping syllables with Level 0 writers by having them clap the syllables in their names and move to hand spelling to focus on beginning sounds. Once Level 1 writers can recognize isolated sounds by hand spelling it's an easy move to finger spelling for Level 2 and 3 writers. Finger spelling transitions easily into supplying a letter for a sound for letter boxes at Levels 2 and 3. Adult underwriting is a great technique for Levels 0 through 2 and may be dropped once children move into Level 3 when most of their writing is easily read. Teaching medial vowels, working with word families, and teaching patterns such as CVC and CVCe are perfect activities for Levels 2 through 4. Word sorting by word families and basic phonics patterns are great activities for Level 4 and lead up to the beginning of second grade level spelling instruction.

Implications

There are four easy implications from this chapter.

1. You should recognize the five levels of emergent writing.

2. Use research-based techniques to help the individual move to the next highest level.

3. Recognize that when you are teaching writing at these levels, you are also teaching reading, so give writing plenty of time in the schedule.

4. Increasing the volume of writing will enhance your students' growth in literacy.

4

Discovery #4: You Need Good-Quality Instructional Resources for Teaching Spelling— The Goodness and Evils of Spelling Books and Alternative Approaches

Once the child completes Phase I and unlocks the complex alphabetic code for English spelling, he or she must enter Phase II (generally a period of several years from second to eighth grade). Adding correct spelling entries to the dictionary in his or her brain is one important goal for literacy. During this time, the child studies spelling. Correct spellings are added to the existing meaning and sound representations in the brain's neural word module for specific words so that correct spelling of a word may be accessed automatically. For many children, the most efficient way to increase the ability to spell correctly and automatically is to study words explicitly, a fact that, according to research, is incontrovertible (Allal 1997; Peters 1985). There have been theories refuting the need to teach spelling explicitly, but to my knowledge, there are no empirical research studies to support them (see Allal 1997; Needels and Knapp 1994).

In this chapter, we consider various methods for teaching spelling and the resources that support spelling instruction. No matter what method is used, it behooves us to begin with five general guidelines for teaching word-specific knowledge successfully:

1. Follow a curriculum.

2. Use research-based techniques.

3. Focus on the right words and patterns at the right time.

4. Differentiate instruction.

5. Connect spelling and word study to reading and writing.

It is a good idea to start with these guidelines when assessing methods and materials for spelling.

1. Follow a curriculum.

Teaching spelling should not be hit or miss. Based on my analysis and synthesis of research, I believe a spelling curriculum is needed to provide continuity and consistency in instruction and to provide the teacher with needed resources. In the absence of a curriculum, teachers are more likely to focus on the wrong words or patterns at particular stages of development, or they may not know what words and patterns children have already been taught and spend too much time going over unnecessary material. When the curriculum is unspecified, teaching spelling tends to be sloppy, inefficient, and sometimes nonexistent. In today's over-crowded curriculum, with teachers jockeying for time to meet the demands of mandates and testing, it is unreasonable to expect teachers to squeeze in spelling without resources and a curriculum. This is especially true because too many educators fail to recognize that spelling is important and therefore neglect this "low order process" or do not teach spelling because spelling is "an altogether disliked component of the school curriculum" (Downing, DeStefano, Rich, and Bell 1984).

2. Use research-based techniques.

Does the teacher employ appropriate research-based techniques, and do the methods and materials used support their use? Useful research-based techniques are reviewed in Chapter 5, and appropriate teaching–learning activities for the second through eighth grade classroom are described.

3. Focus on the right words and patterns at the right time.

Just as we explored the type and timing of instruction in Phase I, it is important to consider the type and timing of instruction during Phase II. Studies of thousands of samples of children's writing reveal particular words and patterns that are needed by writers at particular grade levels based on their likelihood of use (Rinsland 1945; Smith and Ingersoll 1984). Additionally, spelling instructional methods and materials should take into consideration the fact that it is easier to read a word than it is to spell one (Bosman and Van Orden 1997); consequently, word study for reading often may focus on *different* words or patterns than word study for spelling. A common misconception is that spelling words should be pulled from reading, and that lesson objectives for teaching words in reading and spelling should match. But it's more natural to expect children to learn to read many words before they learn to spell them. I often think of the spelling book as the safety net to ensure that words and patterns previously taught for reading or learned by reading are revisited during the harder task of learning to spell them correctly and automatically. Spelling ability, although it connects with reading fluency, is mainly used for writing, and many new words taught as sight words for reading are a grade level harder in difficulty than are the words children should be learning to spell correctly. Most second graders can read *they*, for example, but any second or third grade teacher will tell you many second and third graders can't spell *they* until the correct spelling of the word is taught. Likewise children need to master the respective short- and long-vowel patterns for *hop* and *hope* before we teach them the consonant doubling/e-drop principle for *hopping* and *hoping*. When considering instructional methods and materials, focusing on the right words and patterns at the right time is paramount.

4. Differentiate spelling instruction.

I don't know of any more important principle in our list of guidelines than differentiating instruction. Children enter any classroom with myriad capacities and levels for spelling. At any given time, no two children have the exact same spelling knowledge in their brains—the National Spelling Bee Championships always determines a winner! Teaching methods and resources, therefore, should always allow for multilevel instruction in the mixed-ability classroom. Simply stated, one-size-fits-all spelling instruction doesn't work. Teachers must know each student as a speller—know the child's instructional level for spelling, spelling habits in writing, and whether spelling is relatively easy or whether this student is the one in every five who struggle with spelling. Teachers must match this student with the words and patterns that are just right and select appropriate methods and materials to meet the individual's needs. Instruction is then provided to increase the student's word-specific knowledge. Given the right methods and teaching resources, knowing the child individually and differentiating spelling instruction is a literacy goal that can be accomplished.

5. Connect spelling and word study to reading and writing.

Students may properly spend some time outside the reading and writing blocks focusing on learning to spell, but spelling should always be connected to reading and writing. Dorothy Strickland's idea of whole–part–whole instruction (Strickland 1998)—beginning with whole text, then deconstructing the textual features, and finally applying and transferring these features back into authentic reading and writing— is relevant to spelling instruction. However, in the context of spelling, whole–part–whole instruction may not mean that all spelling words should be pulled from reading or writing, or taught within reading and writing blocks. A two-hour literacy block may have a separate, daily, fifteen-minute time to focus on spelling study and still adhere to whole–part–whole instructional principles as long as connections to authentic reading and writing are made. This seems very much in keeping with spelling researcher Linda Allal's call to coordinate explicit teaching with integrated contextual approaches (1997). The literacy block would likely have at least one hour a day of reading instruction, including time for independent, whole-class, and small-group reading. It would likely have forty-five minutes a day for writing instruction, student writing, and sharing writing. Authentic reading and writing would ensue primarily during these blocks and provide opportunities to connect reading and writing to spelling. But the principle study of spelling, when words are decontextualized, might very well happen in a fifteen-minute block of time each day devoted specifically to spelling and learning word-specific knowledge. Spelling is so important, I believe it needs its own time and maybe even its own book, with ample opportunities to connect the development of word-specific knowledge to authentic reading and writing in much larger daily blocks of time for reading and writing activity.

When focusing on getting new entries of correct spellings into the dictionary in the brain during the second phase of spelling development, it is helpful to consider alternative instructional approaches for learning to spell words. Several instructional approaches may be used to increase the number of entries in the brain's dictionary, ranging from explicit word study to incidental learning from reading and writing. Remarkably, many educators focus on only one approach and often fight over why they think one particular method is better than another. A more reasonable tack might be to combine the features of several alternative approaches, as has been recommended by Allal, whose cross-cultural analysis recommended coordinating explicit teaching with spelling acquisition integrated in text production (Allal 1997). Most approaches now in use fall into the seven categories in Figure 4–1.

The seven methods of teaching spelling are not equally effective. Let's consider the basic strengths and liabilities of each of the seven methods. Thinking about spelling books is a good place to start because Methods 1 and 2 in Figure 4–1 are basically spelling book options. One of the major advantages of spelling books is that they provide teachers with resources for teaching spelling and guide them in the selection of core words for weekly study. Spelling books provide a curriculum for teaching spelling words and systematically organize spelling instruction to make teaching spelling easy. A good spelling book provides the right words at the right time, units of study across grades, a developmental sequence, resources for teaching important spelling patterns or principles, and exercises for consolidating spelling skills. The book may guide the teacher to use research-based techniques and be particularly helpful to teachers who do

1. *Nondifferentiated, explicit word study anchored in word lists*
This is often a one-size-fits-all approach employing the use of a spelling book. A relatively recent development by reading publishers is to embed a one-size-fits-all spelling component in the basal reading program.

2. *Differentiated, explicit instruction anchored in word lists*
This method may employ a spelling book and be anchored in a word list; however, instruction is differentiated by offering *above grade level, on grade level,* and *below grade level* lists for weekly spelling units. Allowing the individual to collect misspelled words in writing may further differentiate the individualized word list study. The student finds and masters words he/she misspells in writing, collecting only those words and patterns deemed important enough to learn. These "need to know" words are generally easier than the student's current instructional level for spelling, and the words have high utility for future use. (*Sarcophagus* and *Tutankhamen*, for example, may be misspelled in the fourth grader's report on Egypt but *not* be added to the weekly spelling list.)

3. *Explicit study of common spelling patterns*
Popularized in recent years by a technique called "word sorting," this method engages children in learning the common patterns found in English spelling. Children sort words according to pattern until they recognize the patterns automatically and form some sense of the probability that a particular pattern is correct.

4. *Incidental learning of spelling by reading*
This method is sometimes referred to as "teaching spelling in context." It is based on the theory that readers and writers learn to spell incidentally.

5. *Focusing on writing and teaching spelling in use*
This method is a combination of incidental learning with the added feature of selected mini-lessons for teaching spelling in the context of writing instruction.

6. *Fad programs*
These programs have little theoretical or research base, but they are often popular among teachers who have no other resources. Sometimes these programs have one or two researched-based features—use of a visualization technique, for example—but they lack comprehensiveness and the theoretical or research base required for overall effectiveness.

7. *"Teacher Choice"*
This is generally a default method used when no resources or instructional training is made available to teachers in a district or school. What generally happens is a smorgasbord of the six techniques cited above with two additional options that may be quite harmful: (1) Teachers sometimes come up with their own very ineffective practices, and (2) some teachers decide that spelling is trivial and stop teaching it altogether.

FIGURE 4–1   Seven Methods for Teaching Spelling

not know how to teach spelling. Well-designed spelling books may help teachers differentiate instruction as well as provide strategies for connecting spelling and word study to reading and writing.

There are a number of liabilities of spelling books, however. Among the most frequently cited are cost and the assumption that spelling knowledge acquired from using spelling books will transfer to more complex reading and writing tasks. Spelling books may be expensive, and the cost may cut into available funds for other teaching resources. Beyond that, they are not teacher-proof. Consider the following observation by Allal (1997), who summarized characteristics of word memorization approaches:

> Study of word lists is very widespread in elementary schools, but many teachers do not apply the principles that assure instructional effectiveness. Ineffective practices include lack of individualization (all students study the same lists), badly designed exercises (students manipulate words without engaging in sufficient spelling practice), and limited content relevance (too much time spent learning low-frequency words rarely used by students in their writing). (136)

I think the greatest liability of spelling books is the dizzying variety from which teachers are forced to choose and the unevenness of the books in comprehensiveness, research base, and scope. Methods 1 and 2 in Figure 4–1 are basically spelling book methods, but there are considerable differences between Method 1 spelling books and Method 2 spelling books and differences in how the books are used, particularly in the content and activities in which the students who use them are to be engaged. Let's compare several spelling books and you can see this discrepancy for yourself.

Method 1 utilizes one-size-fits-all spelling books. These materials bring a spelling curriculum to the literacy program, provide needed resources for teachers, and provide some consistency in helping children develop word-specific knowledge from grade to grade. Too often, however, Method 1 is reduced to rote memorization of arbitrary word lists. The most current iteration of Method 1 is the growing trend among publishers of providing a spelling component—a one-size-fits-all spelling book—with the reading series. While the spelling component of the reading program is appealing because it eliminates the need to buy separate spelling books, the cost is embedded in the cost of the reading program and the materials may be qualitatively inferior.

Spelling books for Method 2 provide for differentiated instruction and tend to be more comprehensive and research-based. The resources are intended to help teachers individualize spelling instruction, utilizing a pretest to determine what words or patterns a child does not know and then adjusting the list of words to be studied to meet the particular child's needs. Although the entire class may focus on a particular pattern or spelling principle in a weekly unit and initially be tested on the same list, different lists are constructed for each student each week based on the student's mistakes on the pretest. The Method 2 book provides above grade-level, on grade-level, and below grade-level words for each weekly unit. Some Method 2 books further individualize spelling using a split-list system to include words the child has misspelled in his or her writing. Individualized word lists can be time consuming, a management nightmare, and daunting for teachers. I demonstrate how easy it is to implement and manage an individualized word list program in Chapter 5.

Even among Method 1 one-size-fits-all spelling components of reading programs, there are wide discrepancies in the materials. For example, some reading programs replace the spelling book with spelling worksheets. Grade 3 of *Reading, Picture This!* (Scott Foresman, 2000), an example of a reading program with a spelling component, includes a full page for spelling in the teacher's edition with each weekly reading unit. The week in which grade three students are assigned to read "Sam and the Lucky Money," they complete a spelling unit entitled "Including All Letters." On Day 1 and Day 5, the teacher is provided a pretest and posttest, respectively, on fifteen words provided in sentences. Words such as *squeeze, chocolate,* and *swimming* are grouped together with no consideration for common patterns or spelling principles. On Days 2, 3, and 4, students complete worksheets entitled "Including All Letters," based on the rather curious idea for the week's lesson, which is stated as "Some words have more letters than might be expected" (Teacher's Edition, Grade 3, Volume Two, 59j). While the material is purported to be research-based and does employ research-based techniques such as word sorting, the word sort for the week, designated in the worksheet for Day 2, is not based on spelling patterns or principles. Rather, the directions say, "Choose the words from the box that have the number of letters shown at the top of each column. Write each word in the correct column" (59j). Students then sort words such as *squeeze, chocolate,* and *swimming* into columns entitled "Words with Eight Letters" and "Words with Nine Letters," which in my view has nothing to do with their spelling. I believe this is a very weak program—a one-size-fits-all spelling book with arbitrary word lists to be memorized, little comprehensive word study, and too many busywork exercises.

Some Method 1 spelling books have more substance but may still pale in comparison to more comprehensive, research-based Method 2 books. If we juxtapose a Method 1 lesson with a comparable Method 2 lesson, it's easier to make a comparison. Both units compared follow a test–study–test format. *Trophies: Spelling Practice Book, Teacher's Edition Grade 4* is an example of a Method 1 spelling component of a reading series. Lesson 21 is comprised of three, 8 × 11.5-inch spelling book pages for a unit entitled, "Words with /er/." The twenty-word spelling list for the week, with words such as *doctor, dollar, power,* and *calendar,* is presented on each of the three lesson pages, which must be copied and distributed by the teacher. In one year of study, a teacher with twenty-five students would copy and distribute over 3,000 sheets of paper for spelling instruction.

The first lesson page in the *Trophies: Spelling Practice Book* has a hand-writing tip and three exercises that I would characterize as busywork: "Write these Spelling Words in alphabetical order"; "Write the Spelling Word that names each picture"; and "Write the following Spelling Words: *motor, hunger, horror, regular.* Use your best handwriting" (78). The next page has a proofreading activity, but then it gives students incorrect and correct forms to sort out, such as *dollar* and *doller*. (I wonder if providing the incorrect visual representation helps children learn the correct form.) Here the student is directed to "Find the word in each pair that looks right" (79). This page also presents a box stating the purpose of Lesson 21: "Guessing and Checking: If you are not sure how to spell a word with the /er/ ending sound, make a guess. Then check to see if you are right." The last page provides two additional activities that I would characterize as busywork—"Word Shapes" (letter boxes with configuration cues) and "Word Scramble," which requires students to unscramble combinations such as *runheg* into *hunger*. With the exception of the proofreading activity, I do not find the activities instructional. The lesson objective directing students simply to "make a guess" seems contrary to good spelling instruction!

Let's compare the unit described above with a comparable unit in a comprehensive, research-based Method 2 spelling book, Zaner-Bloser's *Spelling Connections: Grade 4* (Gentry 2004). It is easy to locate almost the exact same unit, "Unit 21: Schwa-r: er, or" (128) because the unit titles in Method 1 and Method 2 books are often the same, even though the content of the lessons may vary drastically.

In contrast to Lesson 21 in the Method 1 spelling book, the Method 2 book has more teacher resources, providing six student pages with the unit as compared to three. The first page has a twenty-word spelling list for the week, with words such as *gather, tractor, major,* and *together* presented in both manuscript and cursive; a statement of the unit objective; and a word sort activity based on the two lesson patterns—words ending with *-er* and *-or*. Word sorting by pattern is the main research-based activity designed to help the students master the words based on the lesson objective. The objective for the week is stated on the first page as follows: "Remember that the schwa-r is spelled in different ways: er in *water* and or in *major*" (Gentry 2004, 128). Theoretically, sorting the words—a conceptual, auditory, visual, kinesthetic, and tactile activity—helps the child commit the words to automatic recognition and gives the child some sense of the probability that /er/ at the end of a word is spelled *-er* or *-or*. It gives the child experiences visualizing and manipulating words with the target pattern, which is expected to help consolidate the spelling in memory. Notice that this Method 2 book has incorporated Method 3, word sorting, as an integral part of the instructional framework.

Page 2, entitled "Spelling and Vocabulary" (Gentry 2004, 129), provides three activities to make the spelling–meaning connection, with exercises highlighting the list word meanings, highlighting base words, and using the dictionary: "Write the spelling word for each definition. 1. somewhat: to a certain extent; instead" (Answer: rather); "The suffix-*ous* means 'full of' . . . write the spelling word that is the base word for *wondrous*" (Answer: wonder); "Write the spelling words that appear on the same dictionary page as each pair of guide words. Verb—Wed." (Answer: water).

Page 3, entitled "Spelling and Reading" (130), connects spelling to reading with rhyme completions, sentence completions, and solving analogies: "I____what is <u>under</u> the blanket." (Answer: wonder); "If we study____, we can help each other____the words." (Answers: together; master); "Feel is to rough as taste is to____." (Answer: bitter).

Page 4 (131) connects spelling to writing in a proofreading activity and invites students to "Write a Description" based on the proofread model using as many spelling words as possible. Pages 5 and 6 of the lesson entitled "Vocabulary Connections" (132–33) present exercises that present easier words and harder words that fit the unit pattern, including content words from math and geography. Figure 4–2 presents a chart contrasting the two spelling books.

Contrasting a Method 1 and Method 2 Spelling Book	
Trophies • Spelling Practice Book–Grade 4	*Spelling Connections–Grade 4*
Method 1—One-Size-Fits-All	Method 2—Differentiated Instruction
Lack of individualization	Individualization
No word sorting	Word sorting
Badly designed exercises	Well-designed exercises
Cost embedded in the reading series	Must be purchased separately
No publication date, author, or research-base cited	Publication date, author, and research-base cited
Less comprehensive	More comprehensive
Resources must be copied and distributed by the teacher	Resources provided

FIGURE 4–2   Contrasting Spelling Books

Method 3 revolves around systematic study of spelling regularities. This instructional approach is based on systematic study of spelling patterns and engages children in explicit instruction in words out of context. Students observe and compare words based on their patterns in a context guided by teachers. Speed sorting and writing the column sort are the basic consolidation exercises. There are a number of positive aspects to Method 3. Explicit study of common spelling patterns generally has high utility. Lessons are conceptual as opposed to rote memorization. Lessons are multimodal and when implemented properly may lead to automaticity with high-frequency spelling patterns. Sometimes Method 3 is built into the spelling lessons in differentiated instruction spelling books for Method 2, as was the case with the Method 2 illustration presented above. Word sorting is student-friendly and collaborative and the technique has a theoretical base and is supported by some empirical research (Brown and Morris, in press; Zutell 1992a, 1992b). A basic liability, however, is that word sorting takes time, and word sort instruction is often not easily differentiated to meet the individual speller's needs. A second liability is that in some classrooms, whole-group word sorting has replaced individual word study, which, in my view, is an unintended and inappropriate implementation of the technique. A popular manual for word sorting, *Words Their Way*, indicates that the technique was designed to complement the use of any existing phonics, spelling, and vocabulary curricula (Bear, Invernizzi, Templeton, and Johnston 2000, v), but I don't think word sorting works as the entire instructional program for spelling. There are too many words and too much word-specific knowledge that is not related to patterning.

Methods 4 and 5 represent opposing theoretical views to Methods 1, 2, and 3. While Methods 1, 2, and 3 espouse teaching spelling explicitly, Methods 4 and 5 adhere to the theoretical view that spelling comes naturally and is best learned in context. Methods 4 and 5 espouse integrating spelling acquisition in reading and writing and studying spelling in the functional, social, and contextual milieu of reading and writing activities. Method 4 soft-pedals spelling instruction based on the belief that children learn most of their spelling words by reading and writing a lot. Method 5 puts stock in teaching spelling through minilessons that are integrated within the context of writing. These minilessons are to be "anticipated," and "taught off the top of the head," at the "teachable moment" (Laminack and Wood 1996).

Although Methods 4 and 5 obviously make the important connection to reading and writing, there is little research validation of the effectiveness of these methods for teaching spelling. In an even-keeled, unbiased inspection of this issue, researcher Linda Allal (1997) states the research position succinctly: "Approaches integrating spelling acquisition in text production do not yet constitute a well-recognized instructional option validated by long-term empirical research in the classroom" (145). She goes on to report that "the effectiveness of specific approaches [i.e., Methods 1, 2, and 3 in Figure 4–1] for the acquisition of word knowledge has been demonstrated in a sizable number of studies" (148).

Nevertheless, Methods 4 and 5 ushered in a huge anti-textbook movement in the United States followed by an "over the top" backlash. For example, California reportedly adopted Method 4, and in 1989 California's Board of Education banned spelling books from the lists of required texts. About ten years later, *Times* education writer, Elaine Woo, wrote a column appearing on the front page of the *Los Angeles Times*, lamenting the fact that "the state largely abandoned spelling instruction 10 years ago" (Woo 1997, A1). In the article she described an interesting incident in a community sixty miles north of San Francisco, where two dozen letters from eighth graders published in the local newspaper put the community in frenzy over poor spelling. The school had been vandalized and the eighth grade students, all products of Method 4, wrote letters expressing their outrage. Woo reported,

> For starters, the 25 students spelled "vandal" in nearly as many ways. "Dear Vandales," went one letter. "I really think that you were stuped to mess our classrooms.... Our teachers our upseat and so are the students. I think you should rote in_____."
>
> Or, "Dear Vanduls, I hope your happy now that you just cost us thosands of dollars and ruind are new computers...."
>
> Others got "vandals" right but not much else. "We just got are new cumperters," said one. "Yor relly dameg are thing." Scolded another, "I am verey mad at you and it herts to see my teacher's cry. Ther is know punishment that can fix whate hapend." (A1)

Woo, in what some would characterize as an overreaction, may have created revisionist history in citing an illustration of what had happened in California, predicting that it might happen in the whole nation, if the nation opted for Method 4—"the theory that language skills should come naturally," leading teachers to stop teaching spelling directly. Then she reported dramatic drops in test scores:

> On the Iowa Tests of Basic Skills, one of the nation's oldest and most widely used set of standardized exams, elementary school spelling scores rose from the mid-1970s through the 1980s. But the scores have been dropping since 1990.... In California, too, the news is bad. Spelling scores for the second through tenth grades are markedly lower than those for reading, writing and math, according to a review of 1995–96 standardized test results from 1.7 million students. (A18)

Woo ended her article by cautioning her readers that there was a connection between poor reading scores and not teaching spelling: "The truth of that [i.e., abandoning spelling instruction] hit home when a 1994 federal survey on reading ranked California's students at the bottom nationally" (A19). This opinion was reiterated in the article by comments Woo credited to Bill Honig, California's superintendent of public instruction from 1982 to 1993.

In my view, California and other states have never recovered because teachers stopped teaching words. Method 5, the notion of teaching spelling in the context of writing, glorified anecdotally in books such as *Spelling in Use* (Laminack and Wood 1996), was as popular as the California experiment, and again became the recommended procedure adopted by state departments of public instruction for entire states, such as North Carolina. Like Method 4, this method has produced very little success that has been documented. Yet the anti–teaching spelling explicitly methods have led some teachers to stop teaching spelling altogether due to their firmly held personal convictions that spelling is "caught" from reading—an erroneous idea with no research backing (Peters 1985).

In my view, Methods 6 and 7 are the dark sheep among methods currently in use. Some schools or districts have adopted what I characterize in Method 6 as fad programs with no theoretical or research-base whatsoever. One stunningly simplistic idea—"teach only the high-use words" —caught hold and evolved into a commercial giant, metamorphosing over a ten-year period from what I would characterize as a worm of a program to a methodological butterfly. The eventual program had some attractive characteristics, but it still lacked a theoretical or research base beyond the fact that students learn more spelling words when spelling is taught than when spelling is not taught. Some of the fad programs border on the absurd—teaching spelling by cheerleading, using the whole body to shape each letter in a word, for example.

Even more disastrous, in my opinion, than some of the fad programs is what happens in some Method 7 classrooms. Teachers who are given no guidance or resources may be forced by administrators to come up with their own devices for teaching spelling. In some classrooms, it is like giving a scalpel to medical doctors before training them and having them do open-heart surgery. I see teachers cutting at the heart of the literacy program as they perform unwieldy operations with words under the guise of teaching spelling. One well-intentioned first grade teacher in a parochial school had her students memorize *reformation* in the same list with *hat* and *can*. Another first grade teacher gave the little emerging spellers the words *brother* (third grade level) and *through* (about fourth or fifth grade level) the first week in September. I have observed fifth grade teachers pulling inappropriate words from reading material, subjecting students who can not spell *chief, receive, neighbor,* and *weigh* to memorizing words such as *Nefertiti, Tutankhamen, hieroglyphs,* and *sarcophagus*. While a few of the students make 100 percent on the Nefertiti spelling test, they rarely ever use these words again, but leave fifth grade misspelling *chief, receive, neighbor,* and *weigh*.

Of the techniques mentioned above, the direct instruction methods, when properly administered, receive the most research backing for adding new correct spelling entries to the dictionary in the brain (Allal 1997; Gentry 2002; Graham 1983). Clearly, however, a number of other avenues for learning to spell, such as instilling good spelling habits in writing, are important as well.

Implications

1. Research supports methods geared for teaching spelling explicitly.

2. You need alternative methods and quality instructional resources for teaching spelling.

When spelling instruction is addressed comprehensively, a combination of explicit teaching of words, explicit teaching of important spelling patterns, and connecting spelling to writing and reading makes sense. The instruction must be differentiated so that each individual's needs are addressed. Research-based techniques such as using targeted word lists and a pretest can be an efficient means for determining words and patterns an individual needs to know, but these should be used concurrently with observation, assessment, and teaching of spelling in writing.

3. Not all methods and materials are equally effective. In particular, there is great discrepancy in the quality of spelling books for teaching spelling.

Spelling books are widely used in many schools and districts. I believe the selection and use of spelling books is an important consideration when decisions are made regarding the teaching of spelling. The right book can be a powerful resource for teaching spelling. A poor-quality spelling book can be a deterrent. Some expert advice might be helpful for teachers and curriculum committees who are engaged in the selection of spelling books.

Choosing a spelling book is like choosing a fine wine. Did you ever dine at a fine restaurant in the company of exceptional wine tasters and watch the dynamics surrounding the selection of a truly exceptional wine? Usually, everyone glances at the wine list, but often it is passed to the person in the group who is considered the expert—the wine connoisseur. If there is more than one wine connoisseur, an enlightening discussion takes place about grape variety, vintage year, or personal favorites until, with verve and passion, the interlocutors settle on something truly delightful. The conversation might range from discussions about bouquets, lips, and vintages to pricing, with the original first choice being rejected because it lacked nose or had not been brought to its majority with age. It's good to have someone with expert knowledge help make the selection.

Earlier in this chapter I took you on a little "wine tasting" venture for spelling books—we sampled several varieties. I'm a connoisseur of spelling books. I even have an antique spelling book collection with vintages from the early 1800s! I'm also a producer of sorts—I'm the author of several popular series. I'm not sure one could "scientifically prove" who has the best spelling book any more than it would be possible to use science to prove who makes the best bottle of wine. Experts can agree, however, on certain best product characteristics. The following are the various features of spelling books that I believe make them more or less desirable. Like selecting a fine wine, there's a lot to consider in selecting a good spelling book—a dizzying assortment from which to choose and subtleties sometime distinguish the good ones from the poor ones. Here are my top five considerations:

1. Does it have an author and a publication date? Like a fine wine, one often has to look beyond the label. Just because it says "made in France" doesn't mean it's a good wine. Just because the publisher who published your reading program also produced a spelling book doesn't qualify the book as your best choice.

2. What's the cost of the product? The cheapest wines may not be something you want on your dining table. Likewise, the spelling components the reading publishers are "giving away" may not be suitable for the classroom. You should also consider the cost and inconvenience of reproducing copies for students.

3. Can you get by without drinking wine altogether, or without teaching spelling? You may get by without drinking wine but not without drinking water, and teaching spelling for literacy is like drinking water. Water sustains life. Knowledge of words sustains literacy. Have your students drink in the pool of word-specific knowledge regularly and in full volume. It's good for their literacy health!

4. There are certain liquids one should not drink and certain spelling programs one should not use. Don't use one-size-fits-all spelling books, arbitrary word lists, busywork worksheets, or fad programs with simple gimmicks like recycling high-use words without delving into comprehensive word study.

5. Don't drink wine—or anything—to excess and *don't spend too much time with spelling books*. The spelling book is designed to help you teach

spelling quickly and efficiently in about fifteen minutes a day in the literacy block of two to two and one-half hours.

Figure 4–3 is a chart that will assist you in the selection of quality spelling books.

Checklist for Comparison of Spelling Books		
Question	Yes	No
1. Does the program have an author who has demonstrated expertise in spelling instruction? (This is often an indication of the presence or absence of a research base.)		
2. Does the program have a publication date? (Record the publication date in the Yes box.)		
3. Are the theoretical and research bases of the program explicitly stated?		
4. Does the program differentiate instruction?		
5. Is there information included to help adjust for children who speak English as a second language?		
6. Does the program allow for review or recycling words?		
7. Is the teacher required to do lots of work to implement the program because resources are not provided?		
8. Is a developmentally appropriate word list provided?		
9. Does the program supply above, on, and below grade-level words for each weekly unit?		
10. Does the program allow for individualized instruction by allowing children to add misspelled words from their writing to weekly study?		
11. Does the program follow the test–study–test format?		
12. Does the program include research-based techniques? (List them in the Yes box.)		
13. Does the program connect to authentic reading and writing?		

FIGURE 4–3   Checklist for Comparison of Spelling Books

Can you combine the use of word lists, word sorting, and teaching spelling in writing to help each child learn to spell correctly and automatically?

5

Discovery #5: There Is One Best Way to Teach Spelling—Assess and Teach Each Individual— Hooray for Spelling Books!

What if Picasso had only stirred the paint? You can stir up a little spelling instruction here and there, but the true value of spelling assessment and instruction is the picture it paints of each child's word-specific knowledge and the opportunity it provides to increase word-specific knowledge that enhances writing fluency, reading fluency, and speaking ability. This chapter provides research-based techniques into which, like buckets of paint, you can dip your spelling-instruction paintbrush. But if you only do the technique—stir the paint, so to speak—you will not end up with a masterpiece of each child's word knowledge and literacy. You have to apply the technique appropriately to each child just as the artist applies the paint from the pallet to the canvas. Each of the research-based techniques described in this chapter, like buckets of paint, gives you options for achieving your goal. In spelling, the goal is assessing the child's knowledge and habits as a speller, increasing the knowledge and nurturing better spelling habits. The techniques will help you reach the goal of knowing each child as a speller—instructional level, ease of spelling acquisition, spelling habits in writing—and moving the child to a higher level. But you will not be successful if you only stir the paint and fail to make the application relevant to each child that you teach.

The first section of this chapter provides the paint—research-based techniques that good spelling teachers use to do their work. The second section shows you an instructional framework to help you apply the successful teaching of spelling in your classroom.

A lot of research has been conducted on the art of teaching spelling. Many of the techniques listed below relate to the teaching of spelling anchored in word lists. Others are techniques that grew out of developmental spelling theory and out of teaching spelling in the context of writing. The techniques I highlight are a combination of these very important areas of spelling inquiry. Although some consider them theoretically incompatible, I will demonstrate how techniques for explicit teaching of spelling words, word sorting, and techniques focusing on spelling in writing may be used in concert to strengthen any spelling instructional program.

Six Research-Based Techniques to Use with Weekly Word Lists

Six of the research-based techniques that I find most helpful for teaching spelling in the classroom are related to teaching spelling anchored in a word list:

1. Careful word selection

2. Using a pretest–study–posttest format

3. Using a self-correction technique

4. Teaching children how to study unknown words

5. Spelling games and board games

6. Word sorting

Select the Right Words

You can't paint a picture without the paint, and you can't teach spelling without words. English has more words than any other language. How do you decide which ones to teach at your grade level? This is perhaps one of the most important considerations for successfully teaching spelling. Some language arts experts have suggested that it is as easy as leaving it up to the teacher to choose the words and plan a weekly class lesson based on a useful strategy, principle, or pattern. I disagree with this recommendation. What teacher has time to go through the complex process of observing the class in reading and writing, consulting lists of grade-level benchmarks, and then looking through stacks of frequency lists, pattern lists, family clusters lists, double consonants lists, vowel lists, phonogram lists, silent letter lists, contractions lists, compound words lists, suffixes lists, prefixes lists, synonyms lists, antonyms lists, homographs lists, homophones lists, plurals lists, spelling demons lists, clipped words lists, Latin roots lists, Greek roots lists, roots from other languages lists, and lists of portmanteau words and, finally, compile the weekly lesson based on a spelling principle? I find this recommendation entirely uncongenial to teachers!

The selecting process for teaching the right words is entirely too complex and too time consuming to have teachers choose words and implement a weekly spelling unit without the resources typically found in a good spelling book. Of course, teachers should use observation, the student as informant, and reflective decision making to fine-tune the spelling program by differentiating a weekly word list to fit individual and group needs, but selecting all the words and spelling patterns to be studied by twenty-five students for an entire year of their educational career, based on observation with minimal resources, is entirely overwhelming. While teacher-chosen core words might work in some first and beginning second grade classrooms, in which the number of words children are expected to know as readers and writers is relatively small, those who support the well-intended "let the teacher choose the words" option fail to recognize that by the end of second grade, children are expected to read and write *hundreds* of words correctly (Pinnell and Fountas 1998, 266), and word-specific knowledge gets much more specialized. Teachers need resources that help them select the right words and patterns, and that help match each child with words that best suit him or her. They need help determining which words and patterns are most important for a particular grade level. Arbitrary word lists with no coordination of the curriculum between grade levels do not work.

The lists should reflect words and patterns likely to be used by writers at developmentally appropriate grade levels. In a fourth grade lesson on the vowel sounds /ôr/ and /ô/, for example, a good resource might provide a fourth grade core list such as *forgot, bought, nor, haul, ought, forest, sport, thought, daughter, port, sort, record, taught, brought, forth, because, fought, report, forty,* and *caught.* In the same weekly unit, lower level spellers might concentrate on an alternate list of fewer of the easier words listed above, or a lower level list might be provided that contains words such as *form, before, morning, north,* and *story.* Higher performing students might be challenged with *audio, naughty, oriole, toward, dinosaur, audience, author, enormous, important,* and *launch.* All of these words would be provided for the teacher the week fourth grade students studied spelling the vowel sounds heard in *sport* (/ôr /), spelled or; and heard in *haul* (/ô/), spelled in different ways: au in *haul,* aught in *caught,* and in ough in *ought.* Fourth grade writers would be tested to see if they already know these patterns, and, if not, they would be taught (Gentry 2004). This practice connects to writing because all writers, especially fourth graders, use these patterns when they write. It is important that the teacher monitor the students' writing to make sure these decontextualized spelling patterns that are taught are transferring. For example, proofreading activity in Writing Workshop might include a word hunt to see how many words can be found to fit the targeted pattern of the week.

Because research shows that many fifth grade writers confuse ei and ie, spelling study one week in fifth grade might focus on the spelling rule, "Write i before e except after c or when sounded like a as in neighbor and weigh. Weird, their, and neither aren't the same either." Good resources might give teachers words such as *receive, pierce, cashier, neighbor, believe, patient, weight, piece, eighty,* and *frontier* for the grade level speller. Lower level spellers might work with *brief, chief, eighth, field, friend, quiet, reindeer, tried, view,* and *weigh.* Superior spellers might be challenged with *achieve, ceiling, conceit, fierce, mischief, niece, reign, relief, shield,* and *yield* (Gentry, Harris, Graham, and Zutell 1998). Most teachers wouldn't have time to search for these words and group them on their own.

A few Method 5 advocates who are against spelling books have criticized the idea of having the teacher "abdicate her professional judgment to the distant authors of some spelling textbook" (Laminack and Wood 1996, 29). Instead, they advocate shifting the emphasis from words to writing: "Children identify words from their own writing to address in their spelling study; lists are now made with a purpose of discussion and further study rather than for testing. There is an emphasis on teaching and learning strategies for spelling; children are correcting words in their writing by using sources in the room" (37). The "strategies" Laminack and Wood recommend for generating spelling include the following: "First, think about how a word looks. . . . Think about whether the word is a long word or a short word. . . . Is the word like any other words you know? . . . Is the word written nearby? . . . Think about what sound you hear in the word" (65–66). A major teaching technique employed by "wise teachers," according to this Method 5 philosophy (see Figure 4–1), is to "*embed talk about spellings* as words are used throughout the day in *meaningful contexts*" (64). These resources go on to say, "Bill, a fifth-grade teacher, shares his own spelling strategies (such as *i* before *e*) by demonstrating his thinking when he writes on the board in front of his students" (65). As pointed out in Chapter 4, techniques such as these are not supported by research (Allal 1997). I don't know about you, but if I were Bill, I would welcome a resource to give me ie and ei words for working with my fifth grade students, and I would not feel validated as a teacher if I were to be expected to teach spelling to fifth graders off the top of my head!

A great deal of research and many considerations go into the selection of words for good spelling resources. Studies of thousands of samples of children's writing are consulted that show what words and patterns children use in their own writing at each grade level (Rinsland 1945; Smith and Ingersoll 1984). Modern lists are compared with classic lists to determine the enduring importance, permanency, and frequency of the words being chosen. Studies are consulted to consider how often particular words appear in print (Carroll, Davies, and Richman 1971;

Kucera and Francis 1967; Thorndike and Lorge 1944). Other studies consider a word's degree of difficulty, universality, permanence, and application to other areas of the curriculum. Studies such as Gates' "A List of Spelling Difficulties in 3,876 Words" help identify common misspellings at particular grade levels, and studies are used to identify "spelling demons" (Gates 1937). As a spelling author of a commercial program, I consulted twenty-two published word lists to help in the selection of words for the series. Selection of the best words is not an easy task.

Just as a teacher matches "just right books" with children for independent reading, he or she must match the right spelling words with each child. Given resources with choices of words from which to choose, the teacher is like a skillful piano tuner tuning a grand piano, making sure the tone is just right. The teacher also acts as the conductor, motivating, increasing the bravado, bringing out nuances, and selecting heavy or lighter works as needed to enhance the program. The teacher/tuner/conductor is very important in the final orchestration, but no music is made without the right notes, and spelling competency doesn't happen without teaching the right words.

Use a Pretest–Study–Posttest Format

In a comprehensive review of spelling research, Graham (1983) validated the use of the "test–study–test" cycle (Fitzgerald 1953; Yee 1969), anchoring the spelling program in word lists (Graham 1983). In my view, administering a pretest is an efficient way to individualize spelling. In the pretest, each writer in the classroom quickly and easily demonstrates whether or not he or she knows the words or patterns in the week's unit of study. If the core words are known, other words are studied. Because spelling is for writing, it sounds appealing to keep spelling in its context. But as it turns out, that's not very efficient. Think of any roomful of 100 people—they could be second graders, fifth graders, eighth graders, or adults. If it were important to quickly and efficiently assess the spelling of each individual in the group, it would be much better to use a word list and a test than to assess spelling in samples of writing. Word lists and test–study–test should be used simply because they are efficient and leave more time for other parts of the literacy curriculum, such as reading and writing.

Use a Self-Correction Technique

Graham's comprehensive review of spelling research validated the practice of having students correct their own spelling tests. Particularly on the pretest and trial tests, more learning occurs when the student corrects as opposed to having buddies check or the teacher make the corrections. Figure 5–1 presents a self-correction technique that many teachers like.

First follow these steps to take a test.

1. Find a partner and take the test (or the teacher may administer the test).
2. Trade spelling lists. Ask your partner to read your list and tell you if there are any words he doesn't know how to say. Say those words for your partner.
3. Ask your partner to read the first word on your list. Write the word on a piece of paper.
4. When you have completed your list, switch roles.

Now you are ready for Circle Dot.

1. Ask your partner to spell your first word out loud—one letter at a time.
2. As your partner says each letter, draw a dot under every correct letter. If you wrote a letter that is not correct, or it you left out a letter, draw a little circle.
3. Use the circles to see the parts of the word that gave you trouble.
4. Write the word again. Check your spelling with your partner.
5. Keep going until you and your partner have tried every word on your lists.

FIGURE 5–1   Circle Dot

Teach Children How to Study Unknown Words

A systematic technique for learning the correct spelling of words by using a combination of visual, auditory, kinesthetic, and tactile procedures was validated by research by Horn (1954) and reported in Allal (1997).

1. Pronounce each word carefully.

2. Look carefully at each part of the word as you pronounce it.

3. Say the letters in sequence.

4. Attempt to recall how the word looks, then spell the word.

5. Check this attempt to recall.

6. Write the word.

7. Check this spelling attempt.

8. Repeat the above steps if necessary.

A variation of this method that many teachers like, called the Flip Folder, is demonstrated in Figure 5–2.

Use Spelling Games

Using spelling games to supplement but not supplant explicit instruction is compatible with cooperative learning theory and is one of the techniques recommended by Graham (1983), though he does not provide empirical research to validate the use of spelling games. Spelling games

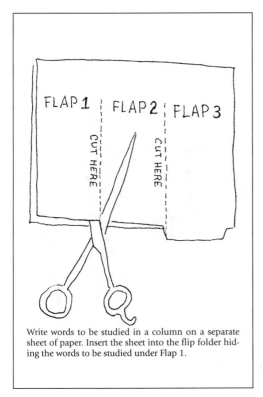

Write words to be studied in a column on a separate sheet of paper. Insert the sheet into the flip folder hiding the words to be studied under Flap 1.

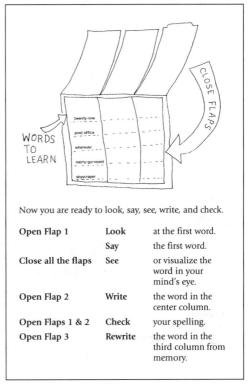

Now you are ready to look, say, see, write, and check.

Open Flap 1	**Look**	at the first word.
	Say	the first word.
Close all the flaps	**See**	or visualize the word in your mind's eye.
Open Flap 2	**Write**	the word in the center column.
Open Flaps 1 & 2	**Check**	your spelling.
Open Flap 3	**Rewrite**	the word in the third column from memory.

FIGURE 5–2   Flip Folder

such as hangman, Scrabble®, and spelling tic-tac-toe are popular with children and teachers and, in my view, should play a role in the elementary spelling program. Children might have the option of using spelling games, working with spelling buddies, to master the words on their individual spelling lists, or to practice word sort patterns. From my experience, I would recommend spelling games as one option for children for studying their words in a period restricted to about fifteen minutes one or two days per week. A particularly popular implementation of spelling games is the use of board games for activities such as Spelling Baseball and Spelling Tic-Tac-Toe. Figure 5–3 presents some popular board game activities.

Word Sorting

Word sorting is an instructional technique based on the systematic study of spelling patterns that grew out of developmental spelling research led by Ed Henderson and his colleagues and students at the University of Virginia (Bear et al. 2000; Henderson 1990; Templeton 1991; Zutell 1992b). Recently, some empirical research has been added to the research base. It focuses on the use of particular word sorts with struggling spellers in

FIGURE 5–3   Examples of Board Games

second grade (Brown and Morris, in press). I believe word sorting is compatible with the brain research implications reported in Chapters 1 and 2 as a way of practicing words and word patterns so that they may be automatically retrieved from memory. In the following activities, speed sorting and writing each column word sort in an individual's word study notebook add to the effectiveness of the activity. A more thorough discussion of word sorting along with "super sorts" for particular grade levels appears in Chapter 7. Figure 5–4 presents three of my favorite word sort activities.

Activity I: Teacher-Led Sort

1. Demonstrate column word sorts to show patterns.

2. Use pocket chart and enlarged word cards or overhead.

3. Teacher and students sort words into patterns.

bush	wood	could	?
bull	crooked	couldn't	sure
helpful	good-bye	shouldn't	
sugar	poor	wouldn't	
put	wooden	should	
	woodpecker	would	
	cookies		
	wool		
	stood		
	hook		
	cook		
	good		
	look		
	took		
	foot		

Activity II: 1-2-3/Make–Sort–Write

1. Make individual word cards.
   Use 8 × 10 paper with grid space for 10 to 16 words.
   Print a word in each space.
   Check the correctness of student copying.
   Cut the words apart.

2. Sort by pattern.
   Child reads down column while teacher or partner checks pattern.

3. Write the spelling words in a word study notebook in columns.

Activity III: Speed Sorts (Shuffle–Sort–Read)

   Use a stopwatch or second hand.
   Player times partner.
   Switch roles.
   Second speed sort/Child tries to beat first time.

Activity IV: Practice Spell Check–Column Formation

   Student calls the words.
   Partner writes the word in the correct column.
   Spellings are checked before partners switch roles.

FIGURE 5–4   Word Sort Activities

Techniques to Connect Spelling to Writing

Personal Spelling Journal

One purpose of the Personal Spelling Journal is to collect spelling words for study from the errors children make in their own writing. Words misspelled on unit tests are also added to the Personal Spelling Journal to be mastered on future weekly word lists. Children are given guidelines to help them self-assess and guide their word choices. They are invited to self-select some of their own spelling words each week as Personal Words to be added to their Core Word list, giving them a sense of ownership and control over their own learning. By paying attention to how they spell words in their writing, they begin to develop better spelling habits in writing.

To set up a Personal Spelling Journal, follow this procedure: Provide or have each student purchase a small spiral notebook specifically for the word journal. Divide the first section of the Spelling Journal alphabetically, allowing two pages for each letter, A through Z. The page may be divided into two columns to accommodate many words per page. This is where students record words they have misspelled in their writing or on a unit spelling test. Additionally, students may also be invited to record new words they want to learn to spell in their Personal Spelling Journal. Following the A through Z section, the remaining pages of the Personal Spelling Journal are where students write the column word sorts they have studied in columns.

The Personal Spelling Journal is the "holding vessel" for words that will eventually be studied in weekly spelling lists. This journal is used every Day 2 when the child constructs his or her list for the week. The child may choose any Personal Words from the Personal Spelling Journal to add to the Core Words misspelled on the Day 1 pretest. These words do not have to fit a particular pattern that is being studied in the weekly unit. A student's weekly list of ten words will generally include about five Core Words and about five Personal Words taken from the Personal Spelling Journal.

When students add a word to their weekly spelling list, they draw a circle around it on the page in the Personal Spelling Journal. Once they learn the word and spell it correctly on the Friday final test, they cross it out. If they misspell the word on the Friday test they do not cross it out but recycle it by adding it to a future weekly list. Figure 5–5 shows this function in a child's Personal Spelling Journal.

Two procedures may be used to find the words a child needs to know how to spell and get them entered into the Personal Spelling Journal. "Green-penning" is a technique the teacher uses to find words, and Student-Found Spelling Words is a technique used by the student. The techniques, as reported in *The Literacy Map* (Gentry 2002), are shown in Figure 5–6.

Choose words from your Personal Spelling Journal to add to your weekly spelling list. When you add a word to your weekly list, draw a circle around it in your Personal Spelling Journal.

When you spell the word correctly on your unit test, cross it out in your Personal Spelling Journal. If you misspell the word on your unit test, add it to another weekly list later and study the word again.

FIGURE 5–5   Personal Spelling Journal

An Instructional Framework for Teaching Spelling

Good teaching of spelling may be coordinated in a teaching framework for teaching words, teaching spelling patterns, teaching strategies, and teaching important spelling principles or rules. Automatic and correct mastery of appropriate words at each grade level aids spellers in developing knowledge and predictability of spelling patterns as well as in developing knowledge of the strategies they need to spell even those words that are not studied formally. In this section, I present a comprehensive framework appropriate for instruction during Phase II, when children are adding new entries to the dictionary in their brains and learning new patterns and strategies that can be generalized, adding new vocabulary words that fit known spelling patterns, and increasing the number of words their brains recognize and retrieve automatically and correctly. The framework includes explicit study of words presented in word list form, explicit study of regular patterns that can be generalized, focus on effective strategies, the teaching of a few good rules, and the connection of spelling with other content areas, with an emphasis on connecting spelling to writing. It includes whole group, small group, and individualized instruction. The framework is *writing based* and includes the study of misspelled words gleaned from children's independent writing. The framework is *individualized,* as it results in each child developing an individual list of unknown spelling words on a weekly basis that he or she learns and adds to the repertoire of automatic and correct spellings in his or her brain. Each week the list to be studied is composed of words a

---

Green-Penning Words

Help children find words they misspell in their writing by green-penning words. Here's how it works. Keep a green ink pen with you at all times. If you spot a developmentally appropriate, high-frequency word misspelled in a student's writing, circle the word, and write it correctly in green at the bottom of the page. Look for these words in anything the child writes. When the child sees a word you have written in green, it means "put this word in your spelling word journal." Green-pen two pages of each child's writing at least once every three weeks. Green penning is for spelling only. Editing is a separate process.

Student-Found Spelling Words

Students should also be responsible for finding misspelled words in their writing for their spelling journals. Once a week, have them follow these student-directed steps:

1. Circle three words on your draft that may be misspelled.

2. "Have a go" at spelling the words again. Try one of these:

> Visualize the word.
>
> Spell it like it sounds.
>
> Spell it by analogy to a spelling you know.

3. Find the correct spelling by asking someone, looking it up, or using a computer spell-checker.

4. Add the correctly spelled words to your list of "Words I Need to Know How to Spell."

FIGURE 5–6   Teaching Activity

particular child has misspelled—either on the pretest or in writing. So the procedure has explicit content relevance. The framework also includes the best features of spelling study anchored in developmentally appropriate word lists. The structured routines are easy to implement, largely managed by the students, inclusive of cooperative learning, and multileveled for the range of spellers in any classroom. The framework has five basic steps:

1. *Assessment.* Teachers or partners administer a pretest based on a weekly unit of Core Words and patterns in a specified, grade-level curriculum. The weekly classroom lesson objective is presented and students are assessed to determine whether they already know the words, patterns, spelling principles, or strategies.

2. *Ownership/Responsibility.* Students build an individual word list of Core Words and Personal Words, using a routine they are taught at the beginning of the year. It consists of a split list format, including both

Core Words from the curriculum (misspelled on the pretest) and Personal Words collected in their Personal Spelling Journals. Each week the child's list contains words misspelled on the pretest and words they should know (i.e., words that are easier than their instructional level) but have misspelled in their writing.

3. *Relevance.* Personal Spelling Journals become vehicles for making the spelling–writing connection. Misspelled words are gleaned from writing or recycled through the Spelling Journal. Not only is the Spelling Journal an excellent record-keeping device, responsibility for adding words to the journal constantly keeps writers in the habit of checking their writing for misspelled words and collecting them. Correcting spelling in writing naturally becomes a good habit.

4. *Teaching.* Spelling is taught explicitly, and new words and patterns are learned each week.

5. *Competency/Accountability/Accomplishment/Contextual Authenticity.* Students are expected to learn new words each week and are held accountable for this expectation. Words spelled correctly on the final spelling test are recycled through the Personal Spelling Journal. During the writing block, decontextualized spelling is integrated back into authentic writing as student writers edit and are guided to focus intently on the words and patterns they have studied in spelling over the past several weeks. For example, a writing checklist for editing used by third graders in Writing Workshop connects directly to decontextualized word study in Spelling Workshop and might look like Figure 5–7, reflecting four weeks of spelling study. Notice that the student had completed units in spelling over the pevious four weeks on double consonants + *y*, adding *–ing* to words ending in *e*, adding *–ing* and doubling the consonant, and contractions.

Thus Whole–Part–Whole instruction not only comes full circle, but continues to revolve. Connecting spelling to writing maximizes a natural transfer from words learned in spelling lessons to correct spelling in writing. Teachers should not assume that the transfer will occur without efforts to make the connection.

In summary, anchor the program in a classroom lesson objective for each week, systematize spelling instruction, differentiate three levels for teaching/learning the concept (high, grade-level, low), individualize student word lists, and include individual need-to-know words that the student has misspelled in writing.

Getting Ready to Implement Your Spelling Program

Begin the year with one spelling group. Allow several weeks to (1) enable students to learn the routines of the spelling block and to (2) complete

---

Editing Checklist

Author's Name _____

Writing Work in Progress _____

Make your corrections in red.

Capital Letters
_____ Important words in the title
_____ Names (proper nouns)
_____ Beginning of all sentences

Punctuation
_____ End marks (. ? !)
_____ Other marks (, " ")

Sentences
_____ Each sentence is complete (subject and predicate).
_____ I have only one *and* in a sentence.

Spelling
_____ Words that I am unsure of are circled.
_____ I checked for double consonants + *y*.
_____ I checked adding -*ing* to words ending in *e*.
_____ I checked doubling *VC* endings + *ed*
            (e.g., -*VCC*ed in *hop, hopped*).
_____ I checked for contractions.
_____ I used my dictionary and my partner to check.
_____ I added circled words to my Personal Spelling Journal.

FIGURE 5–7   Editing Checklist

assessment activities so that you may divide the class into three flexible instructional-level groups:

- Above grade-level spellers
- At grade-level spellers
- Below grade-level spellers

   Teachers should not underestimate the importance of teaching students to work independently. Many teachers begin the fifteen minutes daily spelling block using a fairly traditional test–study–test routine for three to four weeks, with emphasis on determining the three basic groups—above, at grade-level, and below grade-level spellers—and teaching students how to use each routine described in this chapter in detail. It is during this first month that the teacher sets up specific guidelines and routines and takes time for students to practice them so that they learn to do the routines independently. Students learn to take a pretest; use a self-correction technique (e.g., Circle Dot); learn a strategy to study unknown words (e.g., Flip Folder); learn to take a partner test; learn to play various spelling games (though new games may be introduced later in the year); set up and use a Personal Spelling Journal; learn how to find misspelled words in their writing and record them in their Personal Spelling Journal; learn the dynamics of word sorting, including how to participate in a teacher-led sort; learn how to do individual and buddy sorts and how to do speed sorts; and, finally, learn how to recycle any misspelled words on the final test back into the Personal Spelling Journal. Teachers also stipulate a standard for how many words students are responsible for each week and stipulate the times when various routines are expected to occur. Students learn expectations for completing routines in a timely manner. All the routines are practiced with teacher guidance during the first month of school, which is devoted to learning the process and establishing the initial three flexible instructional groups. The time invested in teaching the students to work alone has great returns once students learn how to use each routine in detail.

The following weekly framework has already been introduced in a number of resources (Gentry 2000b, 2002; Gentry and Gillet 1993). The framework presented here has been greatly refined, however, as a result of hundreds of teachers who have used it since it was first introduced as a "spelling workshop" (Gentry and Gillet 1993). It is now a combination of many research-based strategies and of several theoretical stances, and it continues to withstand the test of time, receiving accolades from teachers who use it. For conventional and practical reasons, I favor the five-day unit format, though some teachers extend the time in spelling block and collapse the following framework into a three-day routine. Teachers who do not have spelling books or a curriculum have had to find words and plan the weekly lessons themselves. As described early in this chapter, this is not desirable because it places unrealistic demands on the teachers' time. Nevertheless, the framework still works well for teachers forced into this position. It's effectiveness, however, may vary depending on the teacher's skill in choosing the right words and patterns for Core Word study. Teachers who use spelling resources that may not be of high quality sometimes adjust the provided curriculum as best they can but replace busywork exercises with the recommended procedures in this writing-based, individualized framework. Some teachers with fairly decent developmentally appropriate traditional programs accommodate by adjusting the traditional spelling book to fit the framework presented here.

The Day 1 Routine—Ten-Word Pretest and Self-Correction Check

Day 1 introduces the Core Words and the classroom Lesson Concept or Goal for the week. All students will attend to this concept and be assessed to see whether they already know it.

The teacher needs three, ten-word spelling lists based on the concept being studied for the week: one list on grade level, one list above grade level, and one list below grade level. (A good research-based spelling program generally will provide three levels of word study for each weekly lesson.)

The teacher administers the ten-word pretest to each group in the following manner:

Group 1, your first word is _____. (Use the word in a sentence.)

Group 2, your first word is _____. (Use the word in a sentence.)

Group 3, your first word is _____. (Use the word in a sentence.)

Continue in this manner until all three groups have received their ten-word pretest. Keep in mind that all three groups are flexible in the sense that children move easily from higher to lower groups, depending on their performance on the pretest over a three- or four-week period. For example, a child in Group 2 who makes 100 percent for three weeks in a row may be moved to the higher group. A child who misses more than half the words may be moved to a lower group.

Here is an example of what the pretest looks like in grade 3:

Concept for the Week: Listen to bush, wood, and could. The vowel sound in these words is spelled in different ways: u, as in bush; oo, as in wood; and ou, as in could.

Group 1 (above)	Group 2 (grade level)	Group 3 (below)
bull	bush	book
couldn't	wood	cook
crooked	could	good
good-bye	cookies	hook
helpful	sure	look
poor	wool	put
shouldn't	should	took
wooden	sugar	foot
woodpecker	stood	—
wouldn't	would	—

The next activity on Day 1 is the student-directed self-correction technique, such as Circle Dot. The teacher directs the self-correction technique with one group, and student volunteers direct the check with the other two groups.

1. Listen as I spell your first word out loud—one letter at a time.
2. Put a dot under each correct letter as I say it. If you wrote a letter that is not correct, or if you left out a letter, draw a little circle.
3. Use the circles to see the parts of the word that gave you trouble.
4. At the end of the Circle Dot, you will write the words you missed in a column to be used on Day 2 when you construct your weekly list. Check your spelling with your partner.

The Day 2 Routine—Making the Individual List of Ten Words

The split-list routine using Core Words and Personal Words is easy to teach to students. Start out with a Weekly Spelling List form such as the one in Figure 5–8, with one column for school and another to take home. The student records his or her spelling list for the week in the school column, copies the same list in the home column, and then cuts the list apart. The school list stays at school, and the home list is used for home study. This practice eliminates problems that may arise with lost spelling lists.

  The student first records up to five Core Words chosen from any misspelled words on the Day 1 pretest. (Many teachers have students record this part of the weekly list on Day 1 immediately following Circle Dot.) Words 6 to 10 are Personal Words selected by the student from his or her Personal Spelling Journal. These do not have to fit the unit pattern. Students who get all Core Words correct on the pretest may construct their entire list using Personal Words. If a student only misses three Core Words on the pretest, the remaining words for cells 4 to 10 are Personal

SCHOOL	HOME		SCHOOL	HOME
1.	1.		1.	1.
2.	2.		2.	2.
3.	3.		3.	3.
4.	4.		4.	4.
5.	5.		5.	5.
6.	6.		6.	6.
7.	7.		7.	7.
8.	8.		8.	8.
9.	9.		9.	9.
10.	10.		10.	10.

FIGURE 5–8 Form for Individual List

SCHOOL	HOME
1. *cookies*	1. *cookies*
2. *should*	2. *should*
3. *sugar*	3. *sugar*
4. *stood*	4. *stood*
5. *wool*	5. *wool*

CORE WORDS

SCHOOL	HOME
6. *they*	6. *they*
7. *when*	7. *when*
8. *what*	8. *what*
9. *snake*	9. *snake*
10. *isn't*	10. *isn't*

PERSONAL WORDS

FIGURE 5–9   Making the Individual List with a Split-List Routine

Words. Students who miss more than five Core Words choose any five and complete cells 6 to 10 with Personal Words.

A third grader's list in Figure 5–9 shows Core Words in lines 1 to 5 (missed on the pretest) and Personal Words in lines 6 to 10 (taken from the Personal Spelling Journal). She will cut the list in half and take the home word list for home study, leaving the school list at school so that she never loses her word list.

Why focus on only ten words, one may ask? The answer is that, based on conventional wisdom, ten seems to be the correct number of *unknown* spelling words that works well for students' independent study. It is very important to keep the list short enough to handle in a fifteen-minute daily spelling block but long enough to have substantial impact on the child's growth of word-specific knowledge. When compared with the traditional practice of having children study twenty words each week, ten *unknown* words are appropriate, because children can already spell about half of the words when they are appropriately placed in a traditional twenty-word-list spelling program. Henderson, for example, found that the appropriate instructional level for a basal spelling program is the level at which the student spells about half of the words correctly (Henderson 1981). This being the case, the traditional practice of focusing on twenty words per week is comparable to focusing on ten *unknown* words. I like the more efficient ten-word list because students do not waste time working with words they can already spell, and they manage the list in half the time needed for a twenty-word list. Some second grade teachers have found it works well to begin the second grade year having students construct individual spelling lists with six rather than ten words. Beyond second grade, ten words works very well at every grade level.

Days 3 and Day 4—Word Study Days

Days 3 and 4 are never the same because what happens depends on how the group responds as a whole on the pretest and what the teacher determines to be the best plan for teaching the unit based on this group's pretest feedback—whole-group focus, small-group focus, individual word list focus, or a combination of these three possibilities.

Suppose the weekly unit focuses on an important spelling pattern. If a lot of students do poorly on the pretest and seem to struggle with the pattern, the teacher might conduct a teacher-led sort with the whole class on Day 3 to demonstrate the pattern, teach how the pattern works, and help students learn how to think about various possibilities when applying the pattern in different contexts. Students might make the word sort and practice it as Day 3 homework, and they might do speed sorts with buddies on Day 4 to help consolidate the sort into their repertoire of word-specific knowledge. Here's an example of what a weekly word sort might look like.

bush	wood	could	?
bull	crooked	couldn't	sure
helpful	good-bye	shouldn't	
sugar	poor	wouldn't	
put	wooden	should	
	woodpecker	would	
	cookies		
	wool		
	stood		
	hook		
	cook		
	good		
	look		
	took		
	foot		

Take a moment to revisit the four types of word sort activities in Figure 5–4. Reread the routines for the four types of word sort activities that are described in the figure: Teacher-Led Sorts, Individual or Buddy Sorts (1-2-3-/Make–Sort–Write), Speed Sorts, and Practice Spell Check, using Column Formation Sorts. These are powerful routines for

Spelling Tic-Tac-Toe

1. Find a partner. Draw a tic-tac-toe grid on a piece of paper.

2. Trade spelling lists. Make sure you can read all the words on each other's lists.

3. Decide who will go first. (It's best to take turns going first.) Decide who will use **X** and who will use **O**.

4. Say the first word on your partner's list out loud. Your partner should spell the word out loud while you use his list to check the spelling. If your partner is correct, he should write either **X** or **O** (whichever he is using) on the tic-tac-toe grid. If your partner is not right, spell the word correctly—out loud and one letter at a time—for your partner.

5. Trade jobs. Your partner will say a word from your spelling list and you will try to spell it. If you are right, make an **X** or **O** (whichever you are using) on the board. If you are not correct, your partner will spell your word out loud.

6. Keep taking turns until you or your partner makes three **X**'s or three **O**'s in a line on the board. If you fill up the board before either of you makes a line, start again.

FIGURE 5–10   Spelling Tic-Tac-Toe

teaching patterns, and these activities may be used with whole-class or small groups any week the Core Words and lesson objective focus on a pattern.

Often the teacher may determine that it's best to allow children to work independently or with spelling buddies on Days 3 and 4. A wide range of independent and partner strategies makes it possible for students to choose their own favorite methods of engaging in word study and word learning to focus on their words for the week. Research-based activities described earlier in this chapter may be used, including the Flip Folder, a Look-Say-See-Write-Check individual word study technique (see Figure 5–2), spelling games such as Spelling Tic-Tac-Toe (Figure 5–10), and board games (see Figure 5–3).

The Day 5 Routine—The Partner Quiz

One of the most daunting aspects of using individualized word lists in the classroom is the teacher's concern about how to administer the final test. The secret is the shorter word list. If each student's list has been built with ten unknown words, it is easy for spelling partners to quiz each other and easy for the teacher to quickly check the quiz on the spot, because the partners' completion of the task will be somewhat staggered. The specific guidelines presented here, taught at the beginning of the year, enable partners to administer the final test quickly, accurately, and effectively, addressing issues such as correct reading and pronunciation of another child's list.

1. *Pronunciation.* The test taker is responsible for correct pronunciation of his or her spelling words for the week. Once children construct their word lists on Day 2, they are asked to make sure they can pronounce the words correctly and, if needed, supply the correct pronunciation for their spelling buddy. (Practicing correct pronunciation makes for a good Day 2 spelling homework activity.) If the test giver mispronounces a word, the test taker politely says the correct pronunciation out loud, such as "The correct pronunciation of my spelling word, *asterisk*, is /as′ tēr-isk/."

2. *Reading the Words.* For the final test, test givers are directed to bring any word they cannot read to the teacher, who whispers the word to the student, who then resumes testing. In practice, reading the word is rarely an issue because most test takers already know the words in their lists, having worked with them since Day 2. "You are not sure how to read the word in my list that starts with *a*? Oh, that's *applesauce*" is an example of this dynamic at work in a partner quiz. Some teachers establish spelling buddies earlier in the week so that by Day 5 partners are already familiar with their buddy's words and are more likely to be able to read them.

3. *Preparing the List.* The test taker must prepare the list for the test giver to read. It must be neat and readable. Homophones such as *our* and *hour* are designated with a picture clue to enable the test giver to differentiate the correct word to be spelled by the test taker.

4. Procedure

    1. Partners exchange lists and decide who goes first.
    2. The test giver calls out the word.
    3. If the test giver cannot read the word, he or she asks the teacher to pronounce it.
    4. Once the test is completed, the partners switch roles.
    5. When both tests are complete, partners take the test to the teacher to check on the spot.
    6. Words spelled correctly are crossed out in the Personal Spelling Journal. Words misspelled are not crossed out so that they may be recycled on a later test.

Day 1	10-Word Pretest and Self-Correction Check	Introduce the Core Words. Take the Pretest. Self-correct. Introduce the lesson objective. Put up to 5 Core Words on the individual word list.
Day 2	Individual Word List	Complete adding Core Words. Add Personal Words. Copy List for school and home.
Days 3 and 4	Word Study	OPTIONS: Teacher-Led Sorts Individual or Buddy Sorts 1-2-3/Make–Sort–Write Speed Sorts Practice Spell Check Column Formation Sorts Flip Folder Look-Say-See-Write-Check Spelling Games for Individuals Board Games for Buddies
Day 5	Partner Quiz	Partner quiz Teacher check Record in Personal Journal

FIGURE 5–11   **Five-Day Instructional Framework for the Spelling Block**

Figure 5–11 provides a quick overview of the Five-Day Framework for the fifteen-minute daily spelling block for Phase II spellers.

Implications

The following implications are relatively easy, but they go far beyond simply stirring the paint. Use them as you apply spelling to the broad canvas of literacy and watch a masterpiece of word-specific knowledge transform individual students.

1. Use a research-based curriculum of words and patterns to make it easier for you to implement effective spelling instruction.
2. Use research-based techniques.
3. You really must assess and teach spelling individually. If you employ resources, organization, and well-rehearsed routines, it is easier to individualize spelling instruction than you may think!

6

Discovery #6: The Spelling Pathway to Literacy Is Powerful and Humane

Sometimes spelling reveals the secrets of literacy straightforwardly and at other times in oblique formulations. In both cases the revelations are specific to a single individual and they are deep and powerful. The spelling pathway to literacy goes in two directions—leading children deeper into literacy and, at the same time, leading the teacher to deeper understanding of how literacy develops generally and of how it develops in the individual child. I believe the spelling pathway allows the teacher of literacy to think in three dimensions—the reading dimension, the writing dimension, and the word dimension. There seems to be something about the connectivity of spelling and word-specific knowledge to all literacy acts that is missing in the way that we think about our children as literate beings—something about what they know about words and how they use words. Perhaps American educators have suffered from decades of two-dimensional thinking. Teachers have been trained in teaching reading and writing, but we are not trained to look at how children use words. We do not know what the child's word-specific knowledge reveals. We do not know the impact that word-specific knowledge has on other aspects of literacy development. By adding a spelling dimension, an ability to look at a child's word-specific knowledge and the ability to focus directly on what it tells us about the rest of his or her literacy, we make a powerful connection. We see all aspects of literacy—reading for meaning, writing authentically, speaking articulately, and using words—come together.

In this book I attempt to show that the spelling pathway to literacy is well charted. The new discoveries and a complete understanding of Phase

I and of Phase II spelling reported in this book can be a powerful tool for any teacher in assessing a child's literacy development and in determining what word-specific knowledge has been gained and what needs to be taught. I know of no single more direct, powerful, and relatively easy to accomplish assessment of emergent literacy than to look at a child's writing and let the child's invented spelling tell you what he or she has learned, or not learned, about literacy. The oblique connections are important, too. Of course, there are aspects of literacy other than spelling that will require further investigation, but even obliquely, the spelling pathway can give clues and direct the teacher in the right direction in solving a plethora of literacy problems. Deficiencies in both reading fluency and writing fluency, for example, are often easily predicted by looking at a child's spelling.

Too often the spelling pathway to understanding and teaching literacy is not followed. In my travels across America as an educational consultant, I work directly with children in scores of schools and districts in almost every state. In this chapter I share with you my findings and show how the spelling pathway, a pathway on which too few educators bother to tread, can often lead directly to an individual's literacy needs or reveal, sometimes explicitly, what the student needs to be taught. Too many teachers aren't using the spelling pathway, and in the lives of too many children the spelling pathway to a rich cache of word-specific knowledge that can be subsequently reinvested into more powerful reading ability, easier written expression, and more expert spoken communication is a road not taken.

Teaching spelling is complex. Simply memorizing word lists and doing exercises in spelling books do not develop complete word-specific knowledge. Explicit teaching of spelling must be coordinated with teaching spelling in writing, developing good spelling habits, and paying attention to word-specific knowledge in all aspects of reading. Spelling deserves more dignity and more of our attention than is indicated by its current oversight in elementary education and its relegation to lower order status.

The Children's Individual Paths

The teacher must track each child's individual path to word-specific knowledge. This is a chapter of short vignettes to show you how the spelling pathway can help meet the literacy challenges of children. The episodes and children's work that I share are real. The children are those with whom I have come in contact as I traveled to dozens of states in every region of the nation. Our failure to use the spelling pathway is not isolated. It's not local, statewide, or regional—it's everywhere.

I begin each vignette with a name. Children are individuals, and teaching them in elementary school ultimately reaches a point of one teacher to one individual child; one on one; at minimum, a child and teacher bonding, or, regrettably, in some instances, not bonding. What I have noticed about spelling as a literacy construct is that it is uniquely human and individual. A person's spelling shows qualities characteristic only of that person.

Some of the vignettes I report were very brief encounters. In one of them, I never even met the child. I just analyzed his spelling in a writing sample for his teacher. And although it might seem odd that something meaningful can grow out of a brief encounter over something as seemingly trivial as spelling, this precisely emphasizes the point. Spelling is not trivial! Many of the memories of these encounters—the spelling and writing samples, the children and their stories—stuck with me a long time, and I pondered the issues and circumstances surrounding them from multiple perspectives. I often share this information with teachers.

Teachers sometimes tell me that they marvel at how such a brief encounter may reveal so quickly and clearly exactly what they have been trying to discover about a child's literacy experience for a long time. Why was it so easy for me to pinpoint a literacy problem and come up with just the right solution? The formula is neither secret nor complicated. My answer is that I have no special gift beyond some knowledge of the spelling pathway and the commitment to follow it as a part of my work with children.

In the vignettes that follow think about how you can use the spelling pathway in your work with children and literacy. There's nothing gimmicky about it, and you don't have to turn into a die-hard spelling advocate! The vignettes demonstrate that spelling is an important aspect in the literacy development of each child and they represent a wide range of experiences and levels. They show how teachers who encourage children to invent spelling and write in kindergarten are helping them learn to read. They show how misuse of spelling tests and a lack of understanding about spelling can be disastrous. They show how spelling confirms and extends other important aspects of literacy. They show how spelling connects to both reading and writing fluency at all levels with all students in a wide range of individual differences.

Jonathan—By Inventing Spelling and Writing, He Will Read

It was November, the week after Thanksgiving. I walked into a kindergarten classroom picked at random, introduced myself, and asked how many of the kids liked to read and write. Everyone raised his or her hand! "I need one brave kindergarten person to come write with me in front of a roomful of teachers and principals," I explained. "I'll help you." Lots of kids volunteered and at random I picked one little guy I had never met. His name was Jonathan.

I do this often in kindergarten classrooms and I always get lots of volunteers. Guess who gets nervous—it's the teacher. On the November morning I met Jonathan, the teacher came up to me and said, "Dr. Gentry, we don't write stories until January." But I know that all kids write from the very first day of kindergarten—at minimum they are Level 0 "wavy writers" or "loopy writers," and what I have to do is meet them where they are and help them move to the next level. It's usually a good demonstration for teachers.

In the moments that follow, I try to bond with the child, make him or her comfortable with the situation, and find out something he or she is an expert on to write about. All of these things—bonding with the child, creating a safe and comfortable environment, allowing for self-selected topics—are important at every grade level. Jonathan and I bonded in a conversation over what we did for Thanksgiving and he gave me an elaborate account of his visit to his uncle's house, including detail about his cousins, his dad's DVD, the movies they watched, and everything he ate. I know that children often read or speak at much higher levels than they are capable of writing, so I helped Jonathan set reasonable expectations and I nudged a little bit: "That would make a great story! Why don't you write about what you ate?"

I started by asking Jonathan to write his name because I thought he would be successful and I wanted to know if he knew any letters. He wrote JON.

"That's great!" I told him, and asked him to read it. He looked at *Jon* and said, "Jonathan!"

"Very good!" I said.

"You decided to call this piece 'The Thanksgiving Story,' " I reminded him, and then I showed him where to start by scaffolding the three words in his title, drawing three lines with a yellow marker.

"Start right here," I said, "'The Thanksgiving Story,' " and I pointed to the appropriate yellow line as I pronounced each word. Pointing to the first line I said "the," then I elongated the /th/ sound for him.

He wrote v.

After Jonathan finished the title, I said, "Now tell me what you ate."

"I ate turkey," he said, so I highlighted three lines for those three words under his title. As he wrote the rest of his story, I helped him a bit along the way. "I don't know how to do a G," he told me, so I did one to show him. He completed the piece pretty quickly in front of the adults with a little help from me for an occasional sound or letter. His story is in Figure 6–1 and you can read it. He beamed when he told me this was the first story he had ever written.

What I find most remarkable about Jonathan's story is that it predicts that Jonathan will become a competent reader by the end of first grade. With more opportunities to write in kindergarten, he will more fully develop many of the underlying knowledge sources he needs for reading that are already on display in his writing: knowledge of sounds, more knowledge of the alphabet, phonemic awareness, concept of what a word is, knowledge of phonics, more knowledge of how the English alphabetic

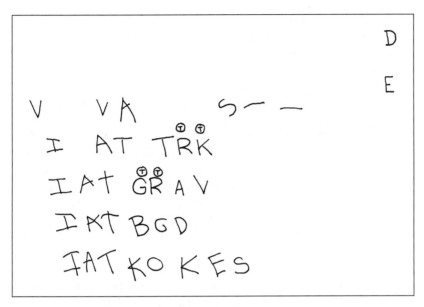

FIGURE 6–1   Jonathan's Story

works in patterns of letters, knowledge of correct spellings of some words, knowledge of predictable story structure, and enthusiasm for using printed language to think and communicate authentically and for his own purposes. Jonathan's teacher was doing a good job. No intervention was needed for this child—just more writing. To witness the first story he had ever written was powerful! I felt like I was watching a baby take his very first steps.

Stephanie—By Inventing Spelling and Writing, She Will Read

Stephanie and I had a wonderful conversation about food. There were about fifty teachers in the room listening and watching us. "This is a great topic for a story!" I exclaimed. "Let's write about food. What do you want to call it?"

"Food I Like," Stephanie answered.

I scaffolded Stephanie's title with three yellow lines and asked her to "read" the lines. She said "Food I like" and made a perfect match with the word that was to go on each line. Then she wrote: F   I   LIEK.

"What's the first food you told me you like?" I asked.

"Pizza," she responded.

Grasping the yellow marker, I made three lines directly under the title and pointed to the appropriate line as I repeated the words she had spoken. "I like pizza."

She wrote it.

"What's next?" I asked.

She said, "I like ice cream."

I made three mores lines and she wrote, "I like ice cream" in kid spelling.

"Finish it," I suggested, and she did. During the process, she paused for each of the food words, and I stretched out the sounds, elongating the prominent sounds. You can see Stephanie's story in Figure 6–2.

At the bottom of the piece, I supplied the Adult Underwriting and we read both the kid spelling and the adult spelling versions over and over together. After a few tries, she could "read" it fluently. I asked her teacher to make sure that Stephanie practiced reading this page of her Kindergarten Writing Journal several times every day independently to her buddies or to a teacher so that whenever I came back—even if it were months from then—she could read it. I pointed out to the roomful of kindergarten teachers that there were more words in her story than in some Level 1 or Level A reading books. Stephanie was very proud of this story.

Stephanie was demonstrating how children learn sounds, how they become aware of phonemes, how they learn letters, and how they learn to write and read, and it was all happening vividly right in front of our eyes. She was also demonstrating that every child is different. She completely stumped me, the spelling guru, with her spelling of *like*. How did this Level 2 speller come up with the *ie*? The LIEK spelling nagged me every time I looked back at her piece, and I puzzled over it for months. If she couldn't spell *pizza* or *ice* in *ice cream*, it was very unlikely she knew a word like *pie*. So where did she get the *ie*? Had she memorized *like* and transposed the letters? I continued to revisit this sample when I worked with teachers. About one year later it struck me. *I* and *E* are the end of her name! S-T-E-P-H-A-N-*I-E*. Children are brilliant and sometimes we are not. The experience reminded to look for the *simple* solution.

The Granddaughter—No Name—Be Careful Not to Misuse the Spelling Test

The spelling pathway to literacy does not comport with a lot of things educators currently do with spelling. For example, assessing a kindergarten child by counting the correctly spelled words on a spelling test without considering what the misspellings indicate about word knowledge and developmental growth is the antithesis of this book. But it happens.

I spoke to a group of educators in a state that is famous for high-stakes testing. At the end of the meeting, a very distinguished educator came up to me and said, "I want to tell you my granddaughter's story." It turns out that the lady was a university professor. She is Hispanic. Her husband is a neurosurgeon. She told me how her own daughter, a medical doctor, called in the midst of tears to report that the granddaughter was being recommended for special education. The granddaughter had

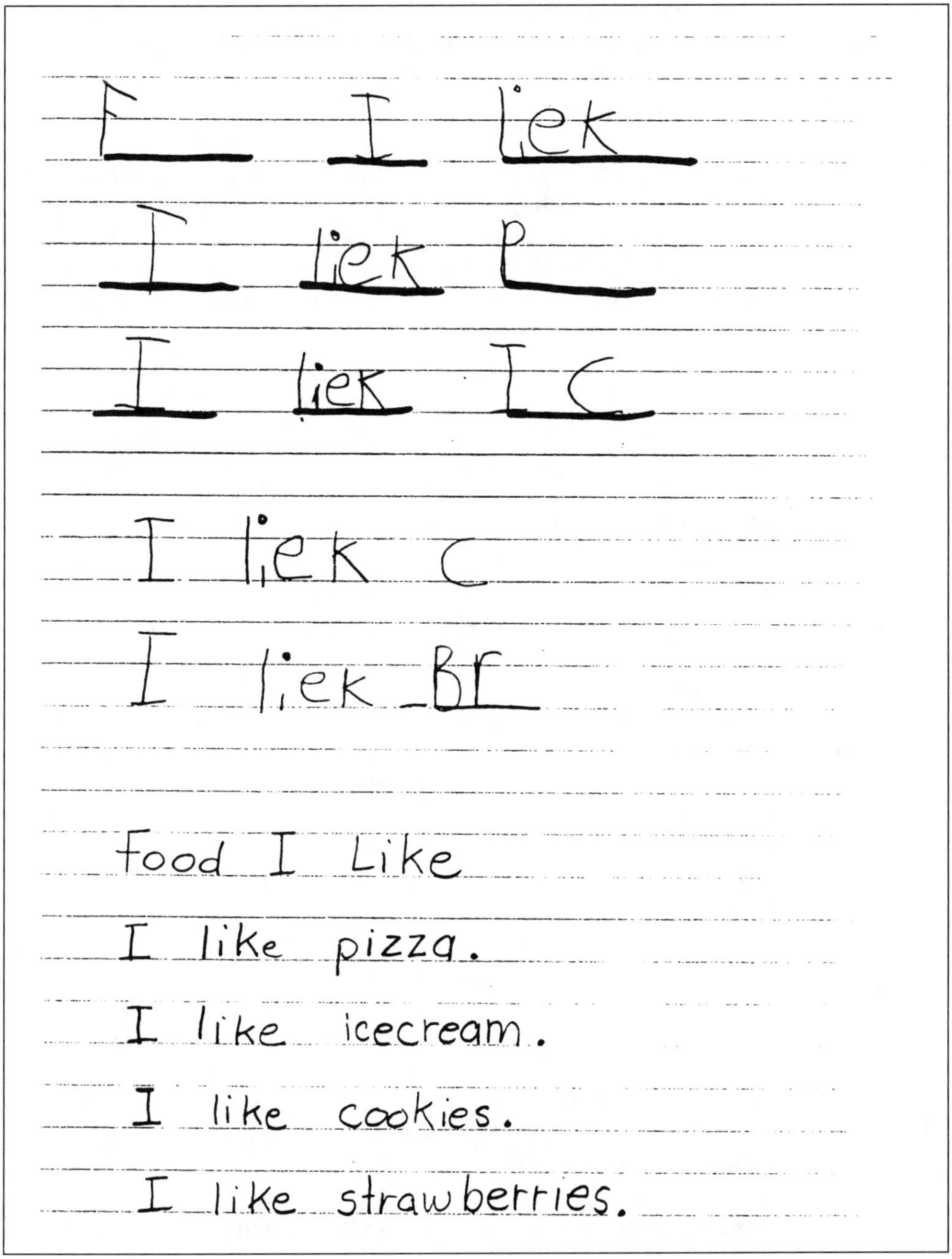

E I liek

I liek P

I liek I C

I liek C

I liek Br

food I Like

I like pizza.

I like icecream.

I like cookies.

I like strawberries.

FIGURE 6–2   Stephanie's Writing

failed the public school kindergarten spelling test, which was part of the required state assessment. The grandmother told me that the grand-daughter was brilliant. The child spoke two languages fluently and could do an eloquent rendition of "The Little Red Hen," always choosing her language to accommodate her listener. The grandmother told me the granddaughter was an independent and discriminating thinker who occasionally put forth some challenges. When the grandmother asked the granddaughter to explain why she refused to give the answers after the teacher read aloud and asked comprehension questions, the grand-daughter responded emphatically, "But Grandmother, the teacher *read* the story to me. She already *knew* the answers!"

I wonder if the granddaughter simply decided that the kindergarten spelling test, like giving answers to the teacher who already *knew* the answers, was inappropriate. The spelling test changed this little girl's life. The parents moved their daughter to a private school.

Sarah—Spelling Consolidates and Extends Phonics Knowledge

Sarah was having great success in first grade. I knew she was from a review of her spelling. I knew it from other observations, too. She read the story in the reading basal with expression and good comprehension. She liked to read and write. It was only September and she could write three line stories like the ones in Figure 6–3.

But why not take Sarah to the next level? I bonded with Sarah in a conversation about pets. She told me a funny story about her dog Chiq-uita, and with a little prompting and the aid of a First-Then-Next-Last story map, the child who had been writing three- and four-line stories wrote a delightful fourteen-line story—in about the same amount of time. Figure 6–4 shows her story, a spelling test I gave her, and the spelling work that grew out of the story.

I noticed that Sarah was still developing her control of short vowels. The little spelling test I gave her confirmed that she already knew correct spelling for important patterns. She spelled *nap, mat, hug, sad,* and *likes* correctly and only misspelled *now*. We worked on *went* and *let* from her story—first by finger spelling and then spelling with letter boxes. She spelled *went* correctly in the letter box, but she spelled *let* as LIT. We prac-ticed reading the *let, bet, get, pet* word family, and I gave Sarah this spelling word sort to practice on her own.

Daniella—Spelling Connects to Reading Fluency

I gave Daniella a spelling test and quickly verified that there was nothing wrong with her spelling. Her parents sat across from us at a large dining table and watched as I worked with this tall, striking second grade stu-dent. One problem, I discovered, was that Daniella was fully one year

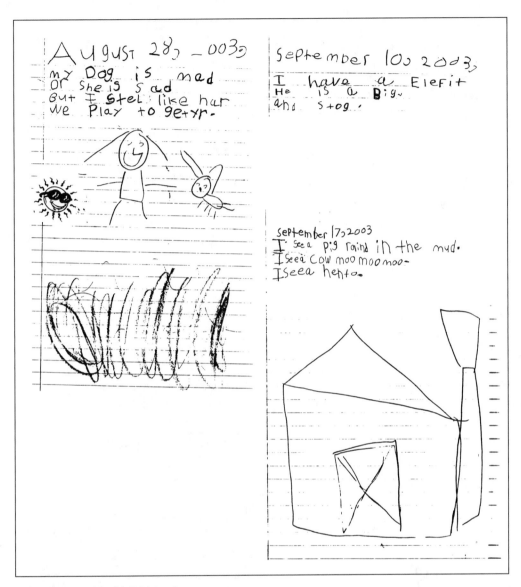

FIGURE 6–3 Sarah's Writing I

behind where the typical second grade student would be expected to function. Daniella's reading, writing, and spelling levels were clearly beginning to middle first grade.

Daniella was born in the United States and first learned to speak English. At three years of age she moved to Hungary and spoke Hungarian. The family moved back to the United States the year Daniella entered kindergarten, and her mother blamed most of Daniella's ensuing

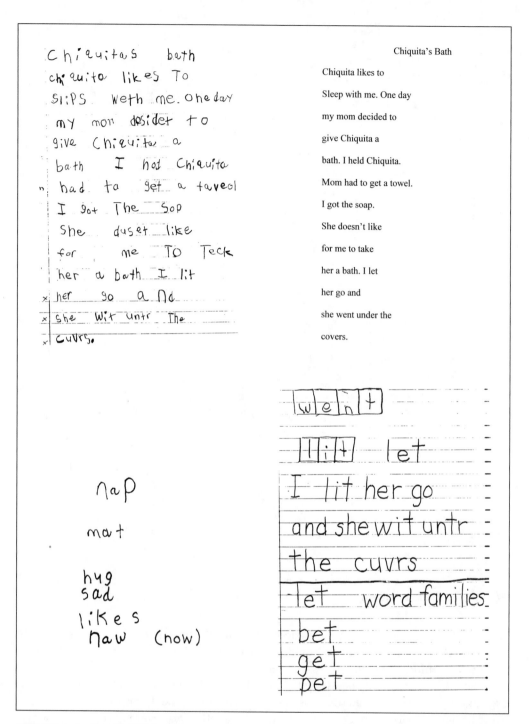

FIGURE 6–4   Sarah's Writing II

academic nightmare on the moving and possible confusion with languages. Seeing no evidence of confusion with languages, I assured the parents that Daniella's fluency in two languages was a plus.

The spelling analysis confirmed that Daniella could read and spell many beginning-level patterns, but her use of these patterns was not being practiced or consolidated so that when reading a book such as Dr. Seuss' *Foot Book*, the reading was slow and halting as she labored word by word. Daniella might just as soon read *foot* as *feet* as she might read *feet* as *foot*. She called out one or the other randomly, paying no attention to the letters in the words.

I tried a hand spelling activity and Daniella caught on immediately. Once she got the hang of it, she noticed the onsets and rime, spelled each word by hand, and pronounced every word I put in front of her correctly. I matched Daniella with easy books with patterns and rhythm that were fun for her, and she practiced until she could read them all perfectly. The repeated readings, choral reading, taped readings, and other fluency work brought on immediate reading improvement.

In just two weeks Daniella mastered nine spelling word sorts from a first-grade-level spelling book. After two weeks of sorting, she did speed sorts and spelled all the words with ease, even though she had been unable to read many of the same words on sight the first day I had worked with her.

Daniella is making fast progress. She will be reading on grade level within six months. Spelling word sorts, fluency work, and matching the type and timing of instruction with what Daniella needed have made a difference.

Chris—The Right Kind of Spelling Helps

My guess is that Chris is dyslexic. I have never met him or heard him read, but I looked at the spelling sample his teacher brought to my seminar and I recognized the classic unexpected spelling patterns that often accompany dyslexia. His teacher was asking for help, and who wouldn't be? Chris is in fifth grade and is at his wit's end with his struggle with literacy and his teacher is frustrated, too.

I analyzed Chris' spelling to try to get some insight into how he thought words worked and offered some suggestions that I thought might help. With 24 percent of the words in the sample misspelled, it was hard for his teacher, or anyone, to know where to start. We had to match Chris with spelling instruction that corresponded to his level of understanding. This intelligent, creative, frustrated writer had no control of vowels at a first grade level. He generated incorrect spellings for basic patterns such as *macks* for *makes*, *was* for *ways* (in *alwas* for *always*), and *sid* for *side* (in *insid* for *inside*). We worked with Chris via email. Figure 6–5 shows my first email to his teacher and demonstrates how we

Hi Jean,

Here's my analysis of Chris' spelling errors plus recommendations:

Chris'	Correct	Chris'	Correct	Chris'	Correct
It	it's	to	too	joly	jolly
Christmass	Christmas	when	one	rufnis	roughness
wanbifl	wonderful	belev	believe	wit	why
yer	year	unrap	unwrap	favrit	favorite
Alwas	always	it	it's	Thackgiving	Thanksgiving
spechel	special	clos	clothes	Howowen	Halloween
ferst	first	evry	every	thew	though
insid	inside	its	it's	Christmass	Christmas
its	it's	macks	makers	all was	always
perfit	perfect	cer	cheer	macks	makes
pik	pick	because	because		
e fens	offense	arrow	around		

About 24 percent of the words in the writing sample are misspelled.

Chris' spelling instructional level is middle to end of first grade. For example, his writing sample illustrates the following lack of word knowledge:

He uses	sid	for	side (insid)
	fit	for	fect (perfect)
	one	for	when
	mack	for	makes
	row	for	round
	wiy	for	why
	ite	for	-it (favorite)
	thack	for	Thanks (Thackgiving)
	wen	for	ween (Halloween)
	was	for	ways (always)
	macks	for	makes

The word sort technique along with lots of practice with speed sorts should help him make dramatic progress.

Start with high-frequency sorts of CVC Short-Vowel Word Families:

cap	hop	not	pet	it	cut
map	mop	hot	wet	fit	but
tap	stop	shot	get	pit	rut
rap	shop	rot	met	sit	but
wrap	pop	cot	set	split	nut
slap				spit	
				bit	
				kit	

FIGURE 6–5   Analysis and Recommendations

Once he can sort, read, and write these automatically, move to CVCe.

cape	hope	Pete	bite	cute	makes
tape	dope	complete	lite	duke	rakes
ape	rope	mete	site	puke	bakes
date	note		spite	nuke	sakes
fate	vote				

thanks
banks
tanks
ranks

Once he can do these automatically, mix sorts with CVC and CVCe such as *cut* and *cute*, *hop* and *hope*. Also show him how *vote* works like *rope*.

Show him how these are the letter combinations he needs to spell big words (polysyllabic words).

For example, have him clap the syllables in *wonderful* and spell each syllable as a chunk:

won-der-ful = wonderful

in-side = inside

fa-vor-ite = favorite

Work with the above curriculum between now and the end of the year. Have his parents work with him on these same sorts at home. Assign him several sort buddies at school. If he learns these he will gain a year in spelling ability in the next five months and you will have him on his way.

Tell Chris that I think he is a great writer and if he would like to share his work, I may put it in one of my books with his permission.

FIGURE 6–5   Continued

began to use spelling instruction to address his frustration with writing fluently.

Pastor—Teach English Spelling to Children Who Speak English as a Second Language

I'm sitting in front of about fifty teachers with Pastor and he looks me dead straight in the eye and makes the most serious and powerful statement of a life plan I have ever heard come out of the mouth of a third grader.

"My Mom and Dad want me to graduate from college." Then he volunteers some more information. "Neither of them got out of school."

I can see in his eyes that they have instilled in him this dream. But will he make it? He can read on grade level in English. He is bright and

mi Bay rabite.
mi grampa gav mi ite.
I tock hume insid.
I gav hume a litol
snac in i letim rin
a litol hillol
I toc hume out sid.
Yin i yint at Sid in it
Yuse stolin   i nu hi
stol it.
   a cid stold it.
uin llir   later i faun
hume. hi vis bige bit i
recg-nisd   him bi a scar.

Mi bay rabite	BITE for -bit (rabbit)	BAY/boy
Mi grampa gav mi ite	GAV for gave	MI/me
I tock hume inside.	ITE for it	
	HUME for him	TOCK/took
	SID for -side (inside)	
I gave hume a litol		
Snac in I letim rin		RIN/run
A litol hillol		HITOL/while
I toc hume out sid	SID for -side	TOC/took
Yin I yint at side init		YIN/when
		YINT/went
		INIT/and it
Yuse stolin I nu hi		YUSE/who
Stol it		
A cid stold it.		CID/kid
Uin llir later I faun		UIN/one
		LLIR/year
Hume. Hi vis bige bit I	BIGE for big	HI/He
		VIS/was
		BIT/but
Recg-nisd him bi a scar.		BI/by

FIGURE 6–6   Spelling and Analysis of a Child Who Speaks English as a Second Language

articulate. He has everything going for him—except English spelling. Look at the story he wrote and my analysis of his spelling in Figure 6–6.

Pastor does not have a spelling disability. He simply has not been taught. Without spelling instruction, will Pastor accomplish his dream?

7

Discovery #7: A Good Spelling Curriculum Makes It Easier to Know Your Students

A spelling curriculum builds on several basic understandings about learning to spell in English. First, there is the obvious consideration that words are not learned one at a time and that large numbers of words may be easier to spell by recognizing common spelling patterns in English. If one can spell *cat*, it's easy to add *rat, fat, sat, mat, at, pat, nat, hat, chat*, and *bat* to one's automatic repertoire—these words share a common spelling pattern. At upper levels, knowledge of Greek and Latin word forms may add thousands of words to a child's vocabulary. An additional consideration is that it's easier to read a word than to spell a word. Beyond that, reading will not necessarily extend exact spelling knowledge, and for many children and adults, spelling is woefully idiosyncratic. There are hundreds of words that I can read automatically, such as *vignette, caveat, from, irritate, before, kitsch, poignant, credence, enigmatic, paradigm, ensure*, and hundreds of names such as my good neighbors the *Lautins* and *Marj*, but I can't spell them. (I commonly misspell them as VINYETTS, CAVEATE, FORM, IRRATATE, BEFOR, KITCH, POINYENT, CREDANCE, INEGMATIC, PARADYM, INSURE, LAUTENS, and MARGE, respectively.) Most readers of this book cannot spell the name of the terrorist group that is responsible for 9/11, even though anyone who reads the newspaper has seen that word hundreds of times, albeit spelled differently by various news organizations. Pastor, who speaks English as a second language (see Figure 6–6), reads English text for me with fluency and comprehension at third grade level, but his knowledge of exact English spelling, as evidenced by such spellings as RIN for *run*, ITE for *it*, LLIR for *year*, and BAY for boy, clearly shows one child's need for experiences that allow him to examine English spelling patterns and learn correctly spelled English words. Almost all of Pastor's reading and writing up to the beginning of third grade was in Spanish, and if he is to be expected to read and write with fluency in English, I believe someone will need to teach him English spelling. All of these examples show that reading is easier than spelling and that spelling is idiosyncratic. This being the case, what kind of curriculum might best support the teaching of spelling words?

A good spelling curriculum is an organized, consistent way of presenting word study that will assist the learner in mastering the basic principles of English spelling. To teach spelling well, spelling researcher Ed Henderson theorized that a basic holding of "memorized" words were required stage by stage or grade by grade for conceptual word-specific knowledge to grow ([1985]1990). For example, if one learns automatic spellings for *hop* and *hope* in first and second grade, it paves the way for easy mastery of *hopping* and *hoping* in third grade. Learning the consonant doubling e-drop rationale for *hopping* and *hoping* in third grade makes it easier to get similar patterns such as *latter* and *later* or *scrabble* and *table*, which share respective double- or single-consonant patterns at syllable junctures. Based on these concepts and a synthesis of word frequency studies, this chapter identifies a basic spelling curriculum for each grade level and the basic pattern and consistency to English spelling that teachers might teach. At the same time, one has to assess spelling individually because spelling is idiosyncratic, and for spellers like Pastor, who may not be ready for grade-level spelling work, there may be a need to learn lower level, more basic patterns and words before being challenged by a myriad of more sophisticated English spellings; that is, there is always a need for the teacher to differentiate instruction.

I believe good spelling instruction always begins with knowing the student as a speller and matching spelling instruction to his or her unique needs. Rather than supplant active decision making, the curriculum or a good spelling book should be a helpful resource for clarifying and enhancing the teacher's decision regarding what the student needs to be taught. The teacher then composes each child's spelling curriculum based on informed decision making. Not only are the instructional resources selected and modified by the teacher, they also allow for selection and modification by the student. Even with the use of a spelling book, as demonstrated in Chapter 5, the curriculum may be teacher and student driven by allowing for individualized word lists and guided self-selection of spelling words that have been misspelled in writing. A good spelling curriculum is both specific and flexible.

A major advantage of a good spelling curriculum and specified word sorting at a particular grade level is that the specified curriculum leads children to grow in word-specific knowledge by showing them where to focus their attention, and word sorting, especially, focuses their attention on the pattern structure of English spelling. Selected word study triggers critical reflections. In the Chapter 5 discussion on teaching the right words, we learned that research on what words and patterns children are likely to use at particular grade levels, common misspellings at particular grade levels, and word frequency in print all help shape the design of a good spelling curriculum.

I believe word sorting has two important instructional functions for developing word specific knowledge—first, learning to *read* words automatically, and second, learning to *spell* words automatically. Because reading is easier than spelling, and children generally can read a word before they can spell it, the first function would be to increase the store of words one reads automatically on sight. One type of word sorting commonly practiced by teachers of emergent reading is the practice of introducing high-frequency word families such as *cat, rat, bat, fat, hat, sat, at*—which is essentially a word sort for sight word recognition. This initial presentation of the word family sort may help the brain react to the word as a pattern, allowing word analysis to become automatic. Once words are recognized automatically on sight, the pattern may be examined further to add correct *spelling* to the neural model for specific words in the brain. Revisiting the pattern a second time with the intent of adding the correct spelling to the child's repertoire of correct spellings may come sometime later than automatic reading recognition. Generally, automatic spelling of many high-frequency words is learned a year later than the reading of the word so that many of the patterns learned in second grade spelling, for example, were learned as new reading vocabulary in first grade. A good spelling curriculum takes this spiraling nature of the growth of word-specific knowledge into account.

In the pages that follow, I provide a general outline of what I would consider to be an appropriate spelling curriculum for elementary school in first grade through eighth grade. (Much of the kindergarten curriculum, which is integrated into the teaching of writing, was presented explicitly in Chapter 3.) Following each grade-level curriculum, I have selected what I call "power word sorts" that trigger critical reflections for writers at the designated grade level. In all cases, spelling must be differentiated. That's why I like the framework presented in Chapter 5. The teacher begins spelling study for the week with a pretest to determine whether writers do in fact know the content of the core curriculum. If this content is known, the child will spend the week focusing on words he or she has misspelled in writing. If the core curriculum content is not known, it will become part of the focus of attention for the week, along with learning other words that the learner has misspelled in writing. A spelling curriculum or a good spelling book is a safety net to ensure that gaining word-specific knowledge is part of the child's literacy experience.

The general grade-level curriculum for spelling that follows includes four components for grade levels one through eight:

- Review of Basic Spelling Principles Applied to More Advanced Vocabulary
- New Spelling Patterns and Principles
- Further Refinement and Extension Appropriate for the Grade Level
- Power Word Sorts

Let's begin with first grade. Keep in mind that word-specific knowledge is learned by degrees. Each year, a review of basic spelling principles is applied to more advanced vocabulary; that is, a previously learned principle is extended to a new application. Each year also engages children with new spelling concepts or major new learning and may include refinement and extension of word-specific knowledge appropriate for the grade level. The listing provided below is certainly not exhaustive but is intended to reflect the basic elements of a core curriculum. The curriculum is based in part on a synthesis and refinement of work reported by spelling researcher Ed Henderson in his classic text *Teaching Spelling* ([1985]1990).

Spelling Curriculum for Grade 1

Revisited Patterns and Concepts Applied to New Vocabulary

Beginning Consonants

Onset and Rime Spelling Patterns as in *bat, cat, fat, sat, mat*

New Spelling Principles—Major New Learning

Major new learning in first grade includes early emphasis on short-vowel patterns. As illustrated in Chapter 3, Level 2 writers often omit the medial vowel (see Figure 3–3). Level 3 writers often invent the short-vowel spelling with an incorrect vowel (see Figure 6–4). They use a letter–name spelling that sounds close to the short-vowel sound: A for short *e*, E for short *i*, I for short *o*, and O for short *u*, as in PAT for *pet*, HET for *hit*, HIT for *hot*, and COP for *cup*. Level 3 writers may invent the spelling of short *a* with an o or a u. For this reason, most first grade spelling programs review kindergarten concepts and then begin a focused emphasis on teaching short vowels, which is a major high-frequency pattern for first grade. In addition, blends, digraphs, and a few high-frequency *e*-marker patterns are introduced.

Short-Vowel Patterns (Teach these first.)

Blends: *st, tr, dr, br, pr*

Digraphs: *sh, th* (*ch, wh*)

Long-Vowel *E*-marker Pattern: *make, time* is introduced

Fine-tuning the Grade 1 Curriculum

Long-Vowel Open-Syllable Pattern, as in *we*, is introduced

Digraph: *ch* contrasted with *tr* in words such as *truck, train, chop*, and *chin*

Blend: *dr* (to replace *jr* invented spelling) in words such as *drop*

Preconsonantal nasal in *stamp, pink, sing, went*

Spelling Curriculum for Grade 2

Revisited Patterns and Concepts Applied to New Vocabulary

Short-Vowel Patterns (CVC becomes solidified and is applied to a growing grade 2 sight vocabulary.)

Blends: *st, tr, dr, br, pr* (applied to a growing grade 2 sight vocabulary)

Digraphs: *sh, th* (*ch, wh, dr, nd, nt, ng*) (applied to a growing grade 2 sight vocabulary)

New Spelling Principles—Major New Learning

In second grade, short-vowel patterns introduced in first grade are revisited a second time, adding expanded second grade vocabulary. The major new learning in second grade is the discovery of pattern relationships in spelling, specifically, the basic CVCe and CVVC patterns for long vowels in single-syllable words. Children leave second grade having mastered myriad one-syllable vowel patterns. They learn that vowel sounds and the pattern of letters used for spelling the vowel sounds within a one-syllable word or a single syllable are related. Some high-frequency two-syllable words are introduced.

Basic One-Syllable Patterns for Each Long Vowel

    CVCe for each long vowel

    CVVC for each long vowel (*nail, bean, peep, pie, boat*)

Introduction of high-frequency two-syllable words such as *funny, mother, happy*

Fine-tuning the Grade 2 Curriculum

-aw, -ow, -ight, -ind, -ood, -ook, -ound, -own

-art , -ore

Double-consonant patterns *ff, ll, ss* (*puff, hill, grass*)

Compound words are introduced (*birthday, into*)

Homophones are introduced, such as *see, sea*

Inflectional endings -*s*, -*ed*, and -*ing* are introduced

Spelling Curriculum for Grade 3

Revisited Patterns and Concepts Applied to New Vocabulary

Unusual Short-Vowel Patterns, as in *bread, healthy, weather*

Basic One-Syllable Patterns for Each Long Vowel

> CVCe for each long vowel (applied to a growing grade 3 sight vocabulary)

> CVVC for each long vowel, including *ai, ea, ee, ie, oa* (applied to a growing grade 3 sight vocabulary)

/s/ spelled *s* or *c*, as in *seven, city, circle*

r-controlled vowels, as in *hair, cheer, earth*

Contractions such as *didn't, weren't*

Spellings of /aw/ in *long, bought, lawn, because,* and *walking*

Ou, ow, oi, oy, as in *found, flower, oil, joy*

W, wh, as in *word, which, where, wheel*

New Spelling Principles—Major New Learning

By third grade, children have developed a large repertoire of correct spellings. Even by the beginning of third grade, over two-thirds of the words they use in writing are typically spelled correctly. Most one-syllable short vowels are spelled correctly and long vowels are spelled with a legitimate long-vowel pattern, albeit not necessarily the correct one. The important principle of meaning constancy is major new learning for grade three (Henderson [1985]1990). Students learn, for example, that *too, two,* and *to* or *by, buy,* and *bye* are allowable patterns for the respective homophones with consistency in spelling once the particular spelling pattern has been affixed with meaning. Meaning constancy is also solidified as they learn that a suffix such as -*ed* is a meaning unit that is always spelled "ed," even though it may be pronounced /t/, /d/, or /id/ in words such as *jumped, dodged,* or *traded.* They learn to expect meaning constancy in prefixes and suffixes and that meaning and letter patterns are related.

New learning includes the following:

Homophones such as *there, their, sent, cent*

Compound words such as *football, grandmother*

Prefixes and suffixes for word building such as *unhappy, preheat, repaint*

Changing *y* to *i* and adding *es*

Plurals -*s* and -*es*, as in *lips, cages, glasses*

Contractions

A second major new principle for grade three is an inchoate understanding of how English spelling works at syllable junctures—particularly, when to double, or not to double, a consonant in two-syllable words.

Double consonants in two-syllable words such as *kitten, rabbit*

Consonant doubling and *e*-drop principle: *hopping* versus *hoping*

Consonant doubling with *er, est*, in words like *hotter, reddest*

Fine-tuning the Grade 3 Curriculum

Stress pattern relationships are introduced

Unstressed syllables -*er* and -*le* are introduced

Spellings for the reduced vowel, schwa, in unstressed syllables are introduced

Capital Letters in words such as *Wednesday, Thursday, March, June*

Unusual spellings of sound, such as /s/ and /j/ as in *circle, pass, giant, join*
-*tch*, as in *hatch, watch, patch*

Consonant blends *scr, spr, str, thr*, as in *scratch, throw*

Spelling Curriculum for Grade 4

Revisited Patterns and Concepts Applied to New Vocabulary

R-controlled vowels in words such as *clerk, shirt, return*

Basic Patterns for Short and Long Vowels are applied to polysyllabic words

> CVCe for each long vowel (applied to polysyllabic words such as *altitude, complete*)

> CVVC for each long vowel, including *ai, ea, ee, ie, oa* (applied to polysyllabic words such as *season, daily*)

Homophones (applied to a growing grade 4 sight vocabulary)

Prefixes and suffixes (applied to a growing grade 4 sight vocabulary)

Compound words such as *good-bye* (applied to a growing grade 4 sight vocabulary)

Contractions such as *you're, haven't*

Adding -*ed*, -*ing*, in no change, double, and e-drop conditions such as *happened, happening, grabbed, grabbing, used, using*

Vowel digraphs *ou, ow, oi, oy,* as in *sound, crowd, spoil, royal*

New Spelling Principles—Major New Learning

Principles of syllable juncture and the basic spelling patterns within poly-syllabic words are learned. Fourth grade is the time for in-depth study of -VC/CV (vowel-consonant/consonant-vowel) and -V/CV (vowel/consonant-vowel) syllable spellings as in *din/ner* and *di/ner*. Stress issues are introduced.

VC/CV (vowel-consonant/consonant-vowel) as in *din/ner*

V/CV (vowel/consonant-vowel) syllable spellings as in *di/ner*

Homographs such as *ré-cord* and *re-córd*

Spelling *-ge* (after long vowel), *-dge* (after short vowel) as in *rage, edge*

Stress pattern relationships are studied:

> Words ending with *-al, -il, -le, -al* such as *metal, pencil, jingle*

> Often confused spellings such as *-en, -in, -on, -an* at the end of a word, such as *kitchen, pumpkin, cotton, cousin, organ*

Possessives *'s* or *s'*

Fine-tuning the Grade 4 Curriculum

Exceptions to meaning constancy such as *sweep* versus *swept*

Three-syllable words

Unusual plurals such as *women, potatoes*

Silent consonants such as in *wrote* and *knife*

Spelling Curriculum for Grade 5

Revisited Patterns and Concepts Applied to New Vocabulary

Meaning Constancy in spelling homophones (applied to a growing grade 5 sight vocabulary)

Meaning Constancy in spelling prefixes and suffixes (applied to a growing grade 5 sight vocabulary)

Meaning Constancy in compound words such as *earthquake* (applied to a growing grade 5 sight vocabulary)

Principles of syllable juncture and the basic spelling patterns within polysyllabic words extended to a growing grade 5 vocabulary, including three-syllable words

VC/CV (vowel-consonant/consonant-vowel), as in *dinner*

V/CV (vowel/consonant-vowel) syllable spellings, as in *diner*

New Spelling Principles—Major New Learning

Fifth grade is a time for consolidating revisited patterns and moving into meaning relationships. Children learn that many words, such as *vane*, *vain*, and *vein*, may only be correctly spelled if their meaning is known. They learn that correct spelling may relate not only to sound, but also to meaning. They begin to get a feel for the numerous contributions to English spelling from other languages. The easier Greek and Latin prefixes such as *bi-* (two) and *tri-* (three) are introduced, paving the way for later, more intensive study of Greek and Latin word elements, which are used to create thousands of English words. This is a good time to learn the *ie*, *ei* rule.

Fine-tuning the Grade 5 Curriculum

Stress pattern relationships studied in light of a growing fifth grade vocabulary

Three-syllable words

Unusual spellings

Spelling Curriculum for Grade 6

Revisited Patterns and Concepts Applied to New Vocabulary

Meaning Constancy in spelling homophones (applied to a growing grade 6 sight vocabulary)

Meaning Constancy in spelling prefixes and suffixes (applied to a growing grade 6 sight vocabulary)

Further study of Greek and Latin roots and words from other languages

Principles of syllable juncture and the basic spelling patterns within polysyllabic words extended to a growing grade 6 vocabulary, including three-syllable words

New Spelling Principles—Major New Learning

In sixth grade, spelling patterns previously introduced are revisited with more advanced vocabulary. Meaning relationships for spelling continue to be studied in sixth grade, with the new element of sound alternation in meaning-related spelling patterns. For example, study ensues with silent letter relationships in words with meaning-related spelling patterns such as *sign* and *signature*, belying the fact that there is more rationality to English spelling than students may realize. The same principle is introduced with vowels in meaning pattern relationships such as *revise* and *revision* where the schwa in the second unaccented syllable of *revision* is predictably spelled with an *i* because the *i* is clearly heard in *revise*. Greek and Latin word elements add to new learning, with new vocabulary words being added through study of base words and root words that receive affixes. Study begins with familiar base words, which students recognize as complete words to which affixes may be added, and proceeds to include root words, which are word parts or meaning elements such as *-phon-* (sound), *-graph-* (writing), *-spect-* (to look), and *-fer-* (to carry), to which affixes are added to create many new words.

Fine-tuning the Grade 6 Curriculum

Stress pattern relationships studied in light of a growing sixth grade vocabulary

Classically derived forms

Spellings of the *-ion* ending

Easily confused endings such as *-able, -ible, -ant, -ent*

Spelling Curriculum for Grades 7 and 8

Revisited Patterns and Concepts Applied to New Vocabulary

Further study of Greek and Latin roots and words from other languages

Principles of syllable juncture and the basic spelling patterns within polysyllabic words extended to a growing grade 7 and grade 8 vocabulary, including technical and academic polysyllablic words

New Spelling Principles—Major New Learning

Seventh and eighth graders are acquiring academic, scholarly, adultlike vocabularies with the addition of many new words from classically derived forms. Spelling study and vocabulary building tend to converge. Students at seventh and eighth grade levels add increasingly advanced layers of word-specific knowledge in word study that often directly integrates with content area study. They continue to study Greek and Latin roots and affixes from which thousands of polysyllabic words may be derived and understood (e.g., *polyunsaturated*). Students learn to break words down into morphemic segments, which give cues to the words' meanings. Spelling is not just important for writing but grows in importance for reading comprehension.

The rather complex concept of consonant assimilation is studied in the seventh and eighth grades. Students learn that some Latin and Greek prefixes change their spellings when added to word roots in order to make them easier to pronounce. For example, *in-* (not) becomes *im-* when added to *-mobile* to become *immobile* because INMOBILE is not an easy English pronunciation. Other examples of assimilated prefixes include *immodest* rather than INMODEST, *account* rather than ADCOUNT, *accept* rather than ADCEPT, *illiterate* rather than INLITERATE. Although seventh and eighth graders may spell words such as *accept* and *irresponsible* correctly, learning that spellings can change to accommodate ease of speech through assimilated prefixes is a new concept.

Fine-tuning the Grade 7 and 8 Curriculum

Stress pattern relationships studied in light of a growing seventh and eighth grade vocabulary

Classically derived forms

Frequently misspelled words

Power Word Sorts

Five power word sorts have been selected for each grade level (see also Appendix B). These word sorts trigger reflection and focus the child's attention on important spelling concepts at the respective grade level. The sorts contain sight words that share the consistencies of the spelling pattern, and the child should recognize these automatically. The pattern or contrasting patterns are the focus of the sort. The child identifies the common elements in the pattern within the word or syllable. The word sort activities presented in Figure 5–4 are recommended for teaching the following word sorts. Each sort should be practiced until the child can successfully complete a speed sort. The correct spellings of the words in the sort should be mastered.

Grade 1	Sort
1–1 Sample Short-Vowel	get—big—but
1–2 Sample Short Versus *E*-marker	cat—make
1–3 Sample Short-Vowel Versus Open-Syllable	me—get
1–4 Sample Mixed Vowel Patterns	cat—bake—day
1–5 Sample Short Versus Long—Mixed Vowels	top—made

Grade 2	Sort
2–1 Sample Short Versus Long Vowel	fed—bee—read

	Sort
2–2 CVCe Versus CVVC	side—nail
2–3 Final Consonants *ll* and *ss*	all—tell—will—boss
2–4 Sample Long Vowel	able—flame—bay—mail
2–5 Compound Words and Homophones	be—into

Grade 3

	Sort
3–1 Endings: *-ed, -ing*	lived—stopping—reading
3–2 *R*-controlled Vowels/ Homophones	chair—pear—care
3–3 Compound Words/ Contractions	yourself—I'd
3–4 Compound Words/ Contractions	aren't—footprint
3–5 -VC/CV Versus -V/CV	sup/per—su/per

Grade 4

	Sort
4–1 Sample Long Vowels, VCe	de/fine—com/plete
4–2 Endings *-on, -an, -in, -en*	cotton—organ—pumpkin—wooden
4–3 Unusual Plurals	woman—women
4–4 Word Building	peace—peaceful—peacefulness
4–5 *-ge, -dge*	edge—judge

Grade 5

	Sort
5–1 The *ie, ei,* Rule	niece—ceiling—weigh—(exceptions)
5–2 Words from Other Languages	(Spanish, French, Italian, other)
5–3 Homophones	board—bored
5–4 Greek and Latin Prefixes	bilingual—midday—triangle—semiannual
5–5 Easily Confused Words	desert—dessert

Grade 6

	Sort
6–1 *Under, over, super, sub*	undercover—overextend—superman —subzero
6–2 -ion	(*-ss* + ion)—(*-ct* + ion)—(*e*-drop + *ion*)–(*-ce* + *ion*)—(*-se* + *ion*)—(*-de* + *sion*)
6–3 Consonant and Vowel Alteration	sign/signature—divide/division

6–4 *-able* and *-ible*	base + *able* (breakable), root + *ible* (horrible), *e*-drop (lovable)— soft *ce/ge* (peaceable)—hard *c/g* (navigable)
6–5 *-ant, -ent*	hesitant—superintendent
Grade 7	**Sort**
7–1 Derived Forms	(prefix/es)—(base word)— (suffix/es) = (derived form)
7–2 Frequently Misspelled Words	(unusual endings)—(unexpected double letters)—(unusual vowel combinations)
7–3 Stress/Double Consonant	confér<u>e</u>nce—confér<u>r</u>ing
7–4 Assimilate Prefix *ad* (to)	accountant—appliance— assortment
7–5 Greek and Latin Roots	*phon(e)*(sound)—*chron* (time)— *tract* (to pull)—*sist* (to stand still)
Grade 8	**Sort**
8–1 Latin Prefixes and Roots	*circum* (around)—*per* (through) —*spir* (to breathe)—*vis* (to see)
8–2 Foreign Spellings	alumna—alumnae—alumnus
8–3 Greek Combining Forms	*arch* (highest)—*crat* (rule, supporter of)—*polis* (city)
8–4 Assimilate Prefix *com, in*	contestant—colleague— correlate—illegal—irresponsible —immortal
8–5 Words from Other Languages	(Native American)—(French) —(German)—(Hindi)—(Dutch)

Postscript

Make a Commitment—Spelling Matters

Are you committed to teaching spelling? On the morning I finished this book, I got up early to write an ending, hoping to meet my deadline. I did not know how the book would end. Before starting my work, I found a sunny spot and relaxed for a moment with my coffee, glancing at the morning newspaper. There on page 5B was an article on spelling! "Big Drop in School Interest Is Spelling a Decline in Bees." Here's the lead: "Spelling bees are being abandoned across Florida by educators who say the schoolhouse tradition eats up class time needed for more important things, including preparation for annual state tests" (Balona 2004). I don't have a great deal of passion for spelling bees, though I don't mind them. They are sometimes great motivators and a boon to spelling instruction. They produce champions—not unlike sport competitions or competitions in music and art. I do have a passion for the *importance* of spelling, however. The article pointed out the problem that I worry about and that prompted me to write this book—not the demise of spelling bees, but that many educators still do not understand the importance of spelling. "Spelling is one of those skills that is not as critical as it used to be because of all the aids we have for spelling" is a quote in the article from the president of the Florida Council of Language Arts Supervisors. The supervisor is wrong. Spelling is *more important* than it has ever been. That is the theme of this book. It is important for the role it plays in our becoming literate. It is important for the role it plays in developing better readers, fluent writers, and articulate speakers. It is important because the word-specific knowledge that grows out of good spelling instruction stays with a person all of his or her life and can be used in whatever he or she does. It is important because we store words in our brains in spellings. *It is important to teach words.* The teacher—and the language arts supervisors—should know that spelling matters. Now that we know more about how spelling works and how to teach it, we should put spelling on a pedestal. Let spelling play an important role in your classroom and take an appropriate place in your literacy instruction. Rather than saying that spelling is not as critical as it used to be, say that it matters. Make a commitment to teach spelling.

Appendix A

Monster Test

Administer the Test

Administer the developmental spelling test printed below to a five-, six-, or seven-year-old. The test is designed for pupils in kindergarten through second grade. When you administer the list, you will obtain spellings that can be categorized roughly into five developmental stages: precommunicative, semiphonetic, phonetic, transitional, and conventional. Once you have analyzed one or two tests, you will be an expert at noticing the same patterns of spelling in young children's free writing.

    Here are the directions. Call out each word; give the sentence provided; and call out the word again. Explain that the words may be too difficult for most kindergarteners and first graders to spell. What you want your pupils to do is invent the spelling or use their best guess at what the spelling might be. Explain that the activity will not be graded as right or wrong, but will be used to see how children think different words should be spelled. Be encouraging, and make the activity challenging, playful, and fun.

    Here are the ten words in the test:

1.	**monster**	The boy was eaten by a monster.
2.	**united**	You live in the United States.
3.	**dress**	The girl wore a new dress.
4.	**bottom**	A big fish lives at the bottom of the lake.
5.	**hiked**	We hiked to the top of the mountain.
6.	**human**	Miss Piggy is not a human.
7.	**eagle**	An eagle is a powerful bird.
8.	**closed**	The little girl closed the door.
9.	**bumped**	The car bumped into the bus.
10.	**type**	Type the letter on the typewriter.

Analyze the Spellings

Table 1 will help you analyze the spellings. Before going further, think about the features that you will look for at each developmental level.

1. *Precommunicative spelling* is the "babbling" stage of spelling. Children use letters for writing words, but the letters are strung together randomly. The letters in precommunicative spelling do not correspond to sounds. Look for spellings such as OSPS for *eagle* or RTES for *monster*. This is Level 1 writing.

2. *Semiphonetic spellers* know that letters represent sounds. They perceive and reliably represent sounds with letters in a type of telegraphic writing. Spellings are often abbreviated, representing initial and/or final sounds. For example, EL for *eagle* and MTR for *monster* are semiphonetic spellings. Only some of many possible semiphonetic combinations are represented in Table 1. This is Level 2 writing.

3. *Phonetic spellers* spell words like they sound. The speller perceives and represents all of the phonemes in a word, though spellings may be unconventional. EGL for *eagle* and BODM for *bottom* are good examples of phonetic spelling. This is Level 3 writing.

4. *Transitional spellers* think about how words appear visually; a visual memory of spelling patterns is apparent. Spellings exhibit conventions of English orthography, such as vowels in every syllable, *e*-marker and vowel digraph patterns, correctly spelled inflectional endings, and frequent English letter sequences. Transitional examples include EGUL for *eagle* and BOTTUM for *bottom*. To distinguish between phonetic spellings (influenced by sound) and transitional spellings

Word	Precommunicative	Semiphonetic	Phonetic	Transitional	Conventional
1. monster	random letters	MTR	MOSTR	MONSTUR	monster
2. united	random letters	U	UNITD	YOUNIGHTED	united
3. dress	random letters	JRS	JRAS	DRES	dress
4. bottom	random letters	BT	BODM	BOTTUM	bottom
5. hiked	random letters	H	HIKT	HICKED	hiked
6. human	random letters	UM	HUMN	HUMUN	human
7. eagle	random letters	EL	EGL	EGUL	eagle
8. closed	random letters	KD	KLOSD	CLOSSED	closed
9. bumped	random letters	B	BOPT	BUMPPED	bumped
10. type	random letters	TP	TIP	TIPE	type

TABLE 1   Possible Test Responses

(influenced by visual conventions) ask the question: Was this word spelled like it sounds (phonetics) or is its spelling analogous to a visually recalled spelling (transitional)? This is Level 4 writing.

5. *Conventional spellers* develop over years of word study and writing. Conventional spelling can be categorized by instructional levels; for example, correct spelling of a general corpus of commonly used words that can be spelled by the average fourth grader would be fourth grade level conventional spelling. Place a given test response in this category if the word is spelled correctly. In words of more than one syllable, if one syllable is spelled at one level and another syllable at a different level, classify the word at the lower developmental level.

Now look at the child's spelling for each word in the developmental spelling test. Find the error type in Table 1 that best matches the child's spelling. Write the appropriate developmental label (precommunicative, semiphonetic, transitional, or conventional) beside each of the ten spellings. Where most of the child's spellings fall is the child's probable developmental level.

Even though ten words is a small sample, this test will reveal the types of developmental errors that a child is likely to make when free writing. Observe invented spellings in the child's free writing to verify the child's level of development. Remember that many of the child's spellings in free writing may be correct. Children who are at lower developmental levels may have memorized spellings for words like *cat*. Children's *misspellings* are what provide snapshots of their minds to reveal their developmental level.

Now you are ready to use what you know about invented spelling. Can you read the adaptation of "The Three Little Pigs" written by a six-year-old first grader and shown in Figure A–1?

This sample may be a challenge for you, especially the ending. Beginning writers often follow the old adage "necessity is the mother of invention" as they space, spell, and punctuate. The six-year-old who wrote this story ran out of space at the end of the page. Insistent that the whole story should fit on one page, she simply squeezed the words wherever they would fit. Be prepared to experience similar kinds of experimentation and risk taking with the spacing, spelling, and punctuation of beginning writers. Remember, they still have lots of discoveries to make.

Now, try reading "The Three Little Pigs" again. This time we've cut it up and pieced it back together to help you decipher it (Figure A-2).

Now that you have read and enjoyed the story, it's time to ask a question of secondary importance: At what level of development is this inventive speller functioning? We could analyze the seventeen

FIGURE A–1   Adaptation of "The Three Little Pigs"

invented spellings in "The Three Little Pigs," but a much more controlled, convenient, and easy way to analyze her spelling is to administer the developmental spelling test. Figure A–3 presents our six-year-old's invented spellings for the Monster Test. (She wrote "The Three Little Pigs" and took the developmental spelling test on the same day.)

Let's walk through an analysis of the spelling word by word. Remember, *phonetic* is spelling by sound, *transitional* is spelling by sight:

1. MONSTR (*monster*) is a bit tricky to classify. MON is a conventional spelling of the first syllable, but STR, with no vowel, is phonetic. Since phonetic is the lower level, let's classify MONSTR as phonetic.

2. UNITD (*united*) represents all the surface sounds of the word. It's in Table 1. Classify UNITD as phonetic.

3. DRES (*dress*) is a transitional spelling (as shown in Table 1). It looks a lot like conventional English spelling.

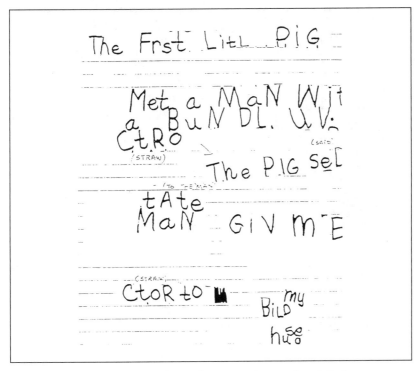

FIGURE A–2 "The Three Little Pigs" in More Conventional Order

4. BOTM (*bottom*) is spelled as it sounds. It doesn't look like English, but all of the sounds are represented. Classify BOTM as phonetic.

5. HIKCD (*hiked*) has all the sounds represented but it doesn't look like English spelling; it is classified as phonetic.

6. HUMN (*human*) is spelled as it sounds. Classify HUMN as phonetic.

7. EGLE (*eagle*) has vowels in every syllable and looks much like English spelling; classify it as transitional. (EGL would be phonetic, but EGLE is more sophisticated, since it uses -*le* at the end of the word, an easily recognized visual pattern.)

8. COELSD (*closed*) is difficult to classify. All six letters in *closed* were used, so it may be transitional. But the letters are scrambled, and some are far from appropriate within-word placement. We would rate this spelling as unclassifiable.

9. BUPT (*bumped*) has a nasal /m/ sound before a consonant, which phonetic spellers systematically leave out. They are in fact spelling by sound. The -*ed* ending is spelled T like it sounds, not like it looks. Classify BUPT as phonetic.

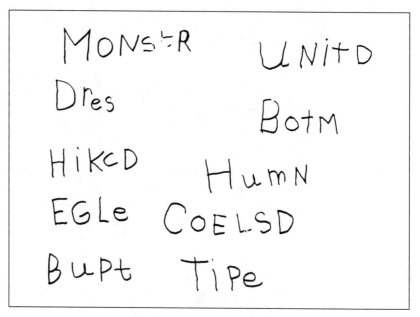

FIGURE A–3   Developmental Spelling Test

10. TIPE (*type*) with its visually inspired *e*-marker pattern is recognized as a transitional spelling (see Table 1).

Here's a quick tabulation of the six-year-old's invented spelling:

- 60 percent phonetic
- 30 percent transitional
- 10 percent unclassifiable

There results indicate that this six-year-old first grader is a phonetic speller who is just beginning to use some transitional strategies. If you were to analyze the invented spellings in her "Three Little Pigs" story you would discover the same developmental level of functioning: thirteen phonetic spellings and four transitional spellings. In both story and test she uses the same strategies, the same pattern for spelling. This is a powerful discovery for a teacher. Knowing her level would enable you to engage this budding writer in developmentally appropriate activities designed to facilitate her growth. You would be able to look at her invented spellings three months hence and determine spelling development or stagnation. You could show parents exactly how she is progressing. You could unlock the next gate or point her in the right direction as she journey's onward down her personal path to literacy—a journey that leads her to new worlds, to a richer and fuller life.

Appendix B

Word Sorts

This section provides five ready-to-go, reproducible power word sorts for each grade level that may also be used to meet an individual's needs. For children who are functioning above or below grade level, appropriate sorts may be matched with individuals by pretesting the words on the word study sheet in a spelling test and assigning those word sorts where the student misspells approximately half of the words in the sort. Follow the procedures in Figure 5–4 for conducting Teacher-Led Sorting, Individual Word Sorting, and Speed Sorting with buddies for each of the word study sheets appropriate for the individual student or grade level.

Have the student cut each word study sheet into word cards and sort the words into columns as indicated at the top of the sheet. After individual practice, remember to have the student write the words in a word

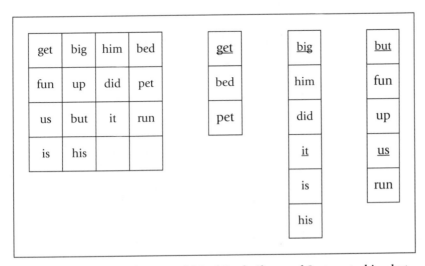

FIGURE A–4   Sample Short Vowel Word Study Sheet and Sort   get—big—but

study notebook in columns. Practice with the selected words and word patterns is designed to help students automatically retrieve the words and patterns from memory. Specified word sorting leads students to grow in word-specific knowledge by showing them where to focus attention on the pattern structure of English spelling.

1–1 Sample Short-Vowel   get—big—but

Cut the word study sheet into word cards. Sort these words into three columns: words like *get,* words like *big,* and words like *but.*

get	big	him	bed
fun	up	did	pet
us	but	it	run
is	his		

1–2 Sample Short Versus *E*-marker   cat—make

Cut the word study sheet into word cards. Sort these words into two columns: words like *cat* and words like *make*.

bat	had	cat	take
hat	can	came	make
at	cake		

1–3 Sample Short-Vowel Versus Open-Syllable   me—get

Cut the word study sheet into word cards. Sort these words into two columns: words like *me* and words like *get*.

me	pet	we	she
let	get	be	he
met	bet		

1–4 Sample Mixed Vowel Patterns   cat—bake—day

Cut the word study sheet into word cards. Sort these words into three columns: words like *cat,* words like *bake,* and words like *day.*

mat	had	at	play
man	take	can	bake
day	came	say	cat
cake	name		

1–5 Sample Short Versus Long—Mixed Vowels   top—made

Cut the word study sheet into word cards. Sort these words into two columns: words like *top* and words like *made*.

had	ride	day	big
he	sheep	top	made
keep	fun	hop	let
us	make		

2-1 Sample Short Versus Long Vowel   fed—bee—read

Cut the word study sheet into word cards. Sort these words into three columns: words like *fed*, words like *bee*, and words like *read*.

fed	bee	sled	see
seed	yes	tree	sweet
wheel	west	read	need
eat	each	mean	keep

2–2 CVCe Versus CVVC   side—nail

Cut the word study sheet into word cards. Sort these words into two columns: words like *side* and words like *nail*.

side	pie	tie	mice
tide	dime	nail	pail
brave	paint	mail	sake
snail	save	trade	tail

2–3 Final Consonants *ll* and *ss*   all—tell—will—boss

Cut the word study sheet into word cards. Sort these words into four columns: words like *all*, words like *tell*, words like *will*, and words like *boss*.

all	ball	tell	will
mall	small	toss	chill
ill	tall	across	boss
miss	spill	yell	hiss

2-4 Sample Long Vowels   able—flame—bay—mail

Cut the word study sheet into word cards. Sort these words into four columns: words like *able*, words like *flame*, words like *bay*, and words like *mail*.

able	afraid	bay	flame
gray	mail	main	paint
ray	spray	wait	place
cage	cape	table	fable

2–5 Compound Words and Homophones   be (homophones)—into (compounds)

Cut the word study sheet into word cards. Sort these words into two columns: words like *be* and words like *into*.

be	into	birthday	bee
meat	something	sea	sometimes
meet	see	homework	right
football	write	anything	herself

3–1 Endings: *-ed, -ing*   lived—stopping—reading

Cut the word study sheet into word cards. Sort these words into three columns: words like *lived*, words like *stopping*, and words like *reading*.

running	closed	coming	hopped
sitting	batted	stopping	cleaning
getting	rented	hopping	having
patted	stopped	reading	called

3–2 *R*-controlled Vowels/Homophones   chair—pear—care

Cut the word study sheet into word cards. Sort these words into three columns: words like *chair*, words like *pear*, and words like *care*.

hair	hare	bear	bare
stare	fair	fare	pair
wear	stair	pear	care
chair	rare	share	scare

3–3 Compound Words/Contractions   yourself—I'd

Cut the word study sheet into word cards. Sort these words into two columns: words like *yourself* and words like *I'd*.

basketball	we're	bookcase	I'd
cardboard	fireplace	flashlight	wasn't
yourself	doghouse	I've	grandfather
can't	achieve	didn't	upstairs

3–4 Compound Words/Contractions   footprint—aren't

Cut the word study sheet into word cards. Sort these words into two columns: words like *footprint* and words like *aren't*.

aren't	doesn't	footprint	hasn't
haven't	highway	they'll	we'll
horseback	you'll	grandmother	didn't
isn't	something	I'll	sunshine

3–5 -VC/CV Versus -V/CV   sup/per—su/per

Cut the word study sheet into word cards. Sort these words into two columns: words like *supper* and words like *super.*

supper	happen	pepper	kitten
super	liter	litter	sudden
dinner	diner	rider	peeper
summer	rabbit	spotted	spider

4–1 Sample Long Vowels, VCe   de/fine—com/plete

Cut the word study sheet into word cards. Sort these words into two columns: words like *de/fine* and words like *com/plete*.

explode	entire	define	arrive
suppose	awhile	complete	reduce
female	surprise	antelope	compose
excite	locate	umpire	alone

4–2 Endings -*on*, -*an*, -*in*, -*en*   cotton—organ—pumpkin—wooden

Cut the word study sheet into word cards. Sort these words into four columns: words like *cotton*, words like *organ*, words like *pumpkin*, and words like *wooden*.

cousin	sudden	common	wooden
dozen	poison	frozen	kitchen
broken	margin	chicken	pumpkin
cotton	organ	harden	linen

4–3 Unusual Plurals   woman—women

Cut the word study sheet into word cards. Sort these words into pairs such as *woman* and *women*.

women	potatoes	goose	woman
pianos	geese	rodeos	tomatoes
piano	tomato	potato	rodeo
child	children	volcano	volcanoes

4–4 Word Building   peace—peaceful—peacefulness

Cut the word study sheet into word cards. Sort these words into three columns: words like *peace*, words like *peaceful*, and words like *peacefulness*.

peace	repay	forget	pay
peaceful	peacefulness	school	preschool
preschooler	restlessly	rest	cheerfully
forgetfulness	prepaying	forgetful	restless

4–5 *-ge, -dge*   rage—judge

Cut the word study sheet into word cards. Sort these words into two columns: words like *rage* and words like *judge*.

edge	judge	village	stranger
rage	dodge	strange	fudge
badge	bridge	strange	grudge
college	danger	knowledge	hedge

5–1 The *ie, ei,* Rule   niece—ceiling—weigh—(exceptions)

I before E except after C or when sounded as A as in *neighbor* and *weigh;* *weird, their,* and *neither* aren't the same *either.*

Cut the word study sheet into word cards. Sort these words into four columns: words like *niece,* words like *ceiling,* words like *weigh,* and words like (exceptions).

achieve	ceiling	their	fierce
mischief	friend	reign	relief
shield	yield	receipt	sleigh
weird	neither	thief	shriek

5–2 Words from Other Languages (Spanish, French, Italian, other)

Cut the word study sheet into word cards. Sort these words into four columns: words from Spanish, words from French, words from Italian, and words from other languages.

karate	macaroni	plaza	yodel
yogurt	guitar	boomerang	chef
buffet	bouquet	parachute	etiquette
diskette	brochure	burro	waffle

5–3 Homophones   board—bored

Cut the word study sheet into word cards. Sort these words into pairs such as *board* and *bored*.

board	bored	manor	manner
isle	aisle	flare	flair
guessed	guest	steel	steal
whose	whose	cell	sell

5–4 Greek and Latin Prefixes   bilingual—midday—triangle—
semiannual

Cut the word study sheet into word cards. Sort these words into four columns: words like *bilingual,* words like *midday,* words like *triangle,* and words like *semiannual.*

biannual	bipolar	midway	bilingual
bimonthly	bisect	midair	midday
midterm	semiprivate	semiformal	semiannual
semifinal	midsummer	trisect	triangle

5–5 Easily Confused Words   desert—dessert

Cut the word study sheet into word cards. Sort these words into pairs or triads: words like *desert* and *dessert*.

vane	dessert	vein	patients
recent	desert	diary	vain
dairy	finally	latter	resent
finely	ladder	coral	patience
corral			

6–1 *Under, over, super, sub*   undercover—overextend—
superman—subzero

Cut the word study sheet into word cards. Sort these words into four columns: words like *undercover,* words like *overextend,* words like *superman,* and words like *subzero.*

undercover	subzero	overextend	underground
superman	submarine	superpower	substandard
overcast	overhead	under-developed	supermarket
superstar	superficial	underweight	submerge

6–2 *-ion*   (*-ss* + *ion*)—(*-ct* + *ion*)—(*e*-drop + *ion*)—
(*-ce* + *ion*)—(*-se* + *ion*)—(*-de* + *sion*)

Cut the word study sheet into word cards. Sort these words into six columns: words ending (*-ss* + *ion*), words ending (*-ct* + *ion*), words ending (*e*-drop + *ion*), words ending (*-ce* + *ion*), words ending (*-se* + *ion*), and words ending (*-de* + *sion*).

expression	affection	education	procession
prediction	congratulation	introduction	expulsion
reproduction	repulsion	erosion	explosion
operation	exception	permission	medication

6–3 Consonant and Vowel Alternation: sign/signature—divide/division

Cut the word study sheet into word cards. Sort these words into consonant and vowel alternation pairs: words like *sign/signature* and words like *divide/division*.

sign	confidence	signature	condemn
composition	condemnation	critic	division
criticize	divide	revise	invite
revision	compose	confide	invitation

6–4 *-able* and *-ible*   base + *able* (breakable), root + *ible* (horrible),
e-drop (lovable)—soft *ce/ge* (peaceable)—
hard *c/g* (navigable)

Cut the word study sheet into word cards. Sort these words into five columns: words with a base + *able* (breakable), words with a root + *ible* (horrible), words with *e*-drop (lovable), words with soft *ce/ge* (peaceable), and words with hard *c/g* (navigable).

breakable	horrible	lovable	peaceable
navigable	readable	terrible	possible
usable	deplorable	serviceable	noticeable
despicable	applicable	inexcusable	profitable

6–5 *-ant, -ent*   hesitant—superintendent

Cut the word study sheet into word cards. Sort these words into two columns: words like *hesitant* and words like *superintendent*.

hesitant	superintendent	ignorant	accountant
insistent	malignant	migrant	contestant
urgent	defendant	consistent	indifferent
applicant	opponent	absorbent	dominant

7–1 Derived Forms   (prefix/*es*)—(base word)—(suffix/es) = (derived form)

Cut the word study sheet into word cards. Break the words down by (prefix) + (base word) + (suffix) = (derived form). Sort the words into three columns: words with prefixes, words with suffixes, and words with both prefixes and suffixes.

thoughtfulness	fearlessness	surprising	disappointment
reappearance	requirement	alphabetical	adventuresome
inability	regardless	requirement	canceling
quarrelsome	precautionary	misunder-standing	resourcefulness

7–2 Frequently Misspelled Words   (unusual endings)—(unexpected double letters)—(unusual vowel combinations)

Cut the word study sheet into word cards. Sort these words into three columns: words with unusual endings (*picnicking*), words with unexpected double letters (*vacuum*), and words with unusual vowel combinations (*bouillon*).

picnicking	vacuum	mimicking	peculiar
maneuver	bouillon	courtesy	pursuit
pursue	breathe	league	initial
curiosity	annually	visually	usually

7–3 Stress/Double Consonant   cónfe̲rence-confér̲ring

Cut the word study sheet into word cards. Sort these words into two columns: words like *conference* and words like *conferring*. Notice how the stress affects when to double or when not to double the consonant.

omitted	occurrence	canceling	compelling
budgeted	compelled	reference	referring
conference	credited	conferred	preference
preferred	inference	inferred	traveling

7–4 Assimilate Prefix *ad* (to)   accountant—appliance—assortment

Cut the word study sheet into word cards. Sort these words into three columns: words like *accountant,* words like *appliance,* and words like *assortment.*

affirm	afford	assurance	assortment
attentive	application	alliance	applaud
accustomed	acclaim	appliance	accomplishment
assimilate	accolade	assemble	accountant

7–5 Greek and Latin Roots   *phon(e)* (sound)—*chron* (time)—*tract* (to pull)—*sist* (to stand still)

Cut the word study sheet into word cards. Sort these words into four columns: words with *phon(e)*, words with *chron*, words with *tract*, and words with *sist*.

distract	retract	abstract	traction
consistent	insistence	resistance	persist
consistency	synchronize	chronology	chronicle
chronic	symphonic	microphone	resist

8–1 Latin Prefixes and Roots   *circum* (around)—*per* (through)—
                                 spir (to breathe)—*vis* (to see)

Cut the word study sheet into word cards. Sort these words into four
columns: words with *circum,* words with *per,* words with *spir,* and words
with *vis.*

circumvent	circumnavigate	circumstantial	circulation
circumlocution	circumspect	perpetrate	persuasion
perforate	persistence	supervision	revisionist
expiration	respiration	perspiration	aspiration

8–2 Foreign Spellings   alumna—alumnae—alumnus

Cut the word study sheet into word cards. Sort these words into groups of related pairs or triads like *alumna—alumnae—alumnus.*

alumna	analyses	alumnus	memoranda
curricula	curriculum	data	phenomena
memorandum	phenomenon	analysis	antennae
datum	antennas	appendix	alumnae
appendices			

8–3 Greek Combining Forms *arch* (highest)—*crat* (rule, supporter of)—*polis* (city)

Cut the word study sheet into word cards. Sort these words into three columns: words with *arch*, words with *crat*, and words with *polis*.

cosmopolitan	metropolitan	metropolis	acropolis
bureaucracy	democracy	autocratic	democrat
anarchy	matriarch	patriarch	monarch
architecture	archives	archetype	aristocracy

8–4 Assimilated Prefix *com-* and *in-* contestant—colleague—correlate— illegal—irresponsible—immortal

Cut the word study sheet into word cards. Sort these words into six columns: words like *contestant,* words like *colleague,* words like *correlate,* words like *illegal,* words like *irresponsible,* and words like *immortal.*

contestant	colleague	confrontation	correlation
constraints	illegality	irresponsible	immaturity
irrational	immortal	illogically	contested
conformity	collegial	irrepressible	immortality

8–5 Words from Other Languages   (Native American)—(French)—
(German)—(Hindi)—(Dutch)

Cut the word study sheet into word cards. Sort these words into five
columns: words from Native American, words from French, words from
German, words from Hindi, and words from Dutch.

snorkel	toboggan	antique	surgeon
boulevard	opaque	faux pas	kindergarten
reservoir	delicatessen	hickory	bungalow
lacquer	etiquette	yacht	finesse

Bibliography

Adams, M. J. 1990. *Beginning to Read: Thinking and Learning About Print.* Cambridge, MA: MIT Press.

Allal, L. 1997. "Learning to Spell in the Classroom." In *Learning to Spell,* edited by C. A. Perfetti, L. Rieben, and M. Fayol, 129–50. London: Lawrence Erlbaum.

Balona, D. 2004. "Big Drop in School Interest Is Spelling a Decline in Bees." *South Florida Sun-Sentinel,* 5B.

Bear, D., M. Invernizzi, S. Templeton, and F. Johnston. 2000. *Words Their Way.* Columbus, OH: Merrill/Prentice Hall.

Blitz, Jeffrey. 2003. *Spellbound.* Documentary movie.

Bodrova, E., and D. J. Leong. 1998. "Scaffolding Emergent Writing in the Zone of Proximal Development." *Literacy Teaching and Learning* 3 (2): 1–18.

Bosman, A. M., and G. C. Van Orden. 1997. "Why Spelling Is More Difficult Than Reading." In *Learning to Spell,* edited by C. A. Perfetti, L. Rieben, and M. Fayol. London: Lawrence Erlbaum.

Brown, J., and D. Morris. In press. "Meeting the Needs of Low Spellers in a Second-Grade Classroom." *Reading and Writing Quarterly.*

Carroll, J. B., P. Davies, and B. Richman. 1971. *Word Frequency Book.* New York: American Heritage.

Clay, M. M. 1993. *Reading Recovery: A Guidebook for Teachers in Training.* Portsmouth, NH: Heinemann.

Coles, G. 2000. *Misreading Reading: The Bad Science That Hurts Children.* Portsmouth, NH: Heinemann.

Downing, J., J. DeStefano, G. Rich, and A. Bell. 1984. "Children's Views of Spelling." *The Elementary School Journal* 85: 185–98.

Ehri, L. C. 1997. "Learning to Read and Learning to Spell Are One and the Same, Almost." In *Learning to Spell,* edited by C. A. Perfetti, L. Rieben, and M. Fayol, 237–69. London: Lawrence Erlbaum.

Elkonin, D. B. 1963. "The Psychology of Mastering the Elements of Reading." In *Educational Psychology in the U.S.S.R.*, edited by B. Simon and J. Simon. Stanford, CA: Stanford University Press.

Embick, D., A. Marantz, Y. Miyashita, W. O'Neil, and K. Sakai. 2000. "A Syntactic Specialization for Broca's Area." *Proceedings of the National Academy of Sciences of the United States of America* 97 (11): 6150–54.

Feldgus, E. G., and I. Cardonick. 1999. *Kid Writing: A Systematic Approach to Phonics, Journals, and Writing Workshop.* Bothell, WA: The Wright Group.

Fitzgerald, J. 1953. "The Teaching of Spelling." *Elementary English* 30: 79–84.

Galperin, P. Y. 1992. "Organization of Mental Activity and the Effectiveness of Learning." *Journal of Russian and East European Psychology* 30 (4): 65–82.

———. 1969. "Stages in the Development of Mental Acts." In *A Handbook of Contemporary Soviet Psychology,* edited by M. Cole and I. Maltzman, 249–73. New York: Basic Books.

Gates, A. I. 1937. *A List of Spelling Difficulties in 3,876 Words: Showing the "Hard-Spots," Common Misspellings, Average Spelling-Grade Placement, and Comprehension Grade Ratings of Each Word.* New York: Bureau of Publications, Teachers College, Columbia University.

Gentry, J. R. In press. "Instructional Techniques for Emerging Writer's and Special Needs Students at Kindergarten and Grade 1 Levels." *Reading and Writing Quarterly.*

———. 2004. *Spelling Connections: Grade 4.* Columbus, OH: Zaner-Bloser.

———. 2002. *The Literacy Map: Guiding Children to Where They Need to Be (4–6).* New York: Mondo.

———. 2000a. "A Retrospective on Invented Spelling and a Look Forward." *The Reading Teacher* 54 (3): 318–32.

———. 2000b. *The Literacy Map: Guiding Children to Where They Need to Be (K–3).* New York: Mondo.

———. 1997. *My Kid Can't Spell!* Portsmouth, NH: Heinemann.

———. 1987. *Spel . . . Is a Four-Letter Word.* Portsmouth, NH: Heinemann.

———. 1985. "You Can Analyze Developmental Spelling." *Teaching K–8* 15: 44–45.

———. 1982. "An Analysis of Developmental Spelling in GNYS at WRK." *The Reading Teacher* 36: 192–200.

Gentry, J. R., K. R. Harris, S. Graham, and J. Zutell. 1998. *Spell It—Write!* Columbus, OH: Zaner-Bloser.

Gentry, R., and J. Gillet, 1993. *Teaching Kids to Spell.* Portsmouth, NH: Heinemann.

Gorman, C. 2003. "The New Science of Dyslexia." *Time,* May 28, 52–59.

Goswami, U. 1996. *Rhyme and Analogy Teacher's Guide.* New York: Oxford University Press.

Graham, S. 1983. "Effective Spelling Instruction." *The Elementary School Journal* 83: 560–67.

Henderson, E. H. [1985] 1990. *Teaching Spelling,* 2nd ed. Boston: Houghton Mifflin.

———. 1981. *Learning to Read and Spell: The Child's Knowledge of Words.* Dekalb, IL: Northern Illinois University Press.

Horn, E. 1954. "What Research Says to the Teacher." *Teaching Spelling* 3: 32.

Hotz, R. L. 1998. "In Art of Language, the Brain Matters." *Los Angeles Times,* 18 October.

Juel, C. 1994. *Learning to Read and Write in One Elementary School.* New York: Springer-Verlag.

Kher, U. 2001. "Blame It on the Written Word." *Time,* March 26, 56.

Kucera, H., and W. N. Francis. 1967. *Computational Analysis of Present-Day American English.* Providence, RI: Brown University Press.

Laminack, L., and K. Wood. 1996. *Spelling in Use: Looking Closely at Spelling in Whole Language Classrooms.* Urbana, IL: National Council of Teachers of English.

Needels, M. C., and M. S. Knapp. 1994. "Teaching Writing to Children Who Are Underserved." *Journal of Educational Psychology* 86: 339–49.

Paulesu, E., J.-F. Demonet, F. Fazio, E. McCrory, V. Chanoine, N. Brunswick, S. F. Cappa, G. Cossu, M. Habib, C. D. Frith, and U. Frith. 2001. "Dyslexia: Cultural Diversity and Biological Unity." *Science* 291 (5511): 2165.

Peters, M. 1985. *Spelling: Caught or Taught?* London: Routledge and Kegan Paul. First ed. published 1967.

Pinnell, G. S., and I. Fountas. 1998. *Word Matters.* Portsmouth, NH: Heinemann.

Report of the National Reading Panel. 2000. "Teaching Children to Read: An Evidence-Based Assessment of the Scientific Research Literature on Reading and Its Implications for Reading Instruction." Washington, DC: National Institute of Child Health and Human Development.

Rinsland, H. D. 1945. *A Basic Vocabulary of Elementary School Children.* New York: Macmillan.

Schlagal, R. 1992. "Patterns of Orthographic Development into the Intermediate Grades." In *Development of Orthographic Knowledge and the Foundations of Literacy: A Memorial Festschrift for Edmund H. Henderson*, edited by S. Templeton and D. R. Bear, 31–52. Hillsdale, NJ: Lawrence Erlbaum.

Scott Foresman *Reading*. 2000. *Picture This! Grade 3, Volume Two*. Glenview, IL: Addison-Wesley Educational Publishers.

Shaywitz, S. 2003. *Overcoming Dyslexia*. New York: Alfred A. Knopf.

Silva, C., and M. Alves-Martins. 2002. "Phonological Skills and Writing of Presyllable Children." *Reading Research Quarterly* 37 (4): 466–82.

Smith, C. B., and G. M. Ingersoll. 1984. "Written Vocabulary of Elementary School Children." *Monograph in Language and Reading Studies* 6. Bloomington: Indiana University Press.

Smith, F. 1978. *Understanding Reading*, 2nd ed. New York: Holt, Rinehart and Winston.

———. 1971. *Understanding Reading: A Psycholinguistic Analysis of Teaching and Learning to Read*. New York: Holt, Rinehart and Winston.

Snow, C., M. W. Burns, and P. Griffin. 1998. *Preventing Reading Difficulties in Young Children*. Washington, DC: National Academy Press.

Stauffer, R. 1980. *The Language–Experience Approach to the Teaching of Reading*. New York: Harper and Row.

———. 1969. *Directing Reading Maturity as a Cognitive Process*. New York: Harper and Row.

Strickland, D. 1998. *Teaching Phonics Today: A Primer for Educators*. Newark, DE: International Reading Association.

Templeton, S. 1991. "Teaching and Learning the English Spelling System: Reconceptualizing Method and Purpose." *Elementary School Journal* 92: 183–99.

Thorndike, E. L., and I. Lorge. 1944. *The Teacher's Word Book of 30,000 Words*. New York: Teachers College Press.

Trophies: Spelling Practice Book. Teacher's Edition Grade 4. [n.d.] New York: Harcourt.

Vygotsky, L. S. 1987. *The Collected Works of L. S. Vygotsky*. Translated by R. W. Rieber and A. S. Carton. New York: Plenum Press. (Original works published in 1934, 1960.)

———. 1978. *Mind and Society: The Development of Higher Mental Processes*. Cambridge, MA: Harvard Educational Press. (Original work published in 1930, 1933, 1935.)

Woo, E. 1997. "How Our Kids Spel: What the Big Deel?" *Los Angeles Times*, 29 May, A1.

Wood, D., J. C. Bruner, and G. Ross. 1976. "The Role of Tutoring in Problem Solving." *Journal of Child Psychology and Psychiatry* 17: 89–100.

Yee, A. 1969. "Is the Phonetic Generalization Hypothesis in Spelling Valid." *Journal of Experimental Education* 37: 82–91.

Zutell, J. 1992a. "An Integrated View of Word Knowledge: Correctional Studies of the Relationships Among Spelling, Reading, and Conceptual Development." In *Development of Orthographic Knowledge and the Foundations of Literacy: A Memorial Festschrift for Edmund Henderson*, edited by S. Templeton and D. R. Bear, 213–30. Hillsdale, NJ: Lawrence Erlbaum.

———. 1992b. "Sorting It Out Through Word Sorts." In *Voices on Word Matters*, edited by Irene Fountas and Gay Su Pinnell, 103–13. Portsmouth, NH: Heinemann.

Suggested Readings

Bear, D. R. 1992. "The Prosody of Oral Reading and Stages of Word Knowledge." In *Development of Orthographic Knowledge and the Foundations of Literacy: A Memorial Festschrift for Edmund Henderson*, edited by S. Templeton and D. R. Bear, 135–88. Hillsdale, NJ: Lawrence Erlbaum.

Colvin, R. L. 1995. "State Report Urges Return to Basics in Teaching Reading." *Los Angeles Times*, 13 September.

Cunningham, P. M., and J. W. Cunningham. 1992. "Making Words: Enhancing the Invented Spelling–Decoding Connection." *The Reading Teacher* 46: 106–15.

Elkonin, D. B. 1974. Psikhologija obuchenijy mladsevo shko' Inika. [*Psychological Issues in Primary Instruction*]. Moscow: Pedagogika.

———. 1973. "U.S.S.R." In *Comparative Reading*, edited by J. Downing, 551–79. New York: Macmillan.

Gentry, J. R. 1995. Spelling Workshop Guide. In *Spell It—Write!* Columbus, OH: Zaner-Bloser.

———. 1977. A Study of the Orthographic Strategies of Beginning Readers. Unpublished doctoral dissertation, University of Virginia, Charlottesville.

Gill, J. 1992. Focus on Research: "Development of Word Knowledge as It Relates to Reading, Spelling, and Instruction." *Language Arts* 69: 444–53.

Goodman, K. 1993. *Phonics Phacts*. Portsmouth, NH: Heinemann.

Hillerich, R. L. 1977. "Let's Teach Spelling—Not Phonetic Misspelling." *Language Arts* 45: 301–07.

Hughes, M., and D. Searle. 1996. "Joe and Elly: Sight-Based and Sound-Based Approaches to Literacy. *Whole Language Umbrella: Talking Points* 7 (4, Spring): 8–11.

Morris, D. 1981. "Concept of Word: A Developmental Phenomenon in the Beginning Reading and Writing Process." *Language Arts* 58: 659–68.

Orton, J. L. 1964. "A Guide to Teaching Phonics." Cambridge, MA: Educators Publishing Service.

Peters, M. 1983. *Essays into Literacy: Selected Papers and Some Afterthoughts.* Portsmouth, NH: Heinemann.

Rasinski, T., and R. Oswald. In press. "Making and Writing Words: Constructivist Word Learning in a Second-Grade Classroom."

Read, C. 1975. *Children's Categorizations of Speech Sounds in English.* Urbana, IL: National Council of Teachers in English.

Richgels, Donald J. 1995. "Invented Spelling Ability and Printed Word Learning in Kindergarten." *Reading Research Quarterly* 30 (1): 96–108.

Routman, R. 1996. *Literacy at the Crossroads.* Portsmouth, NH: Heinemann.

Schlagal, R. 1989. "Constancy and Change in Spelling Development." *Reading Psychology* 10: 207–32.

Stanovich, Keith E. 1993. "Romance and Reality." *The Reading Teacher* 47: 280–91.

Templeton, S. 1992. "New Trends in an Historical Perspective: Old Story, New Resolution—Sound and Meaning in Spelling." *Language Arts* 69: 454–63.

Wilde, S. 1992. *You Kan Red This! Spelling and Punctuation for Whole Language Classrooms, K–6.* Portsmouth, NH: Heinemann.

Yopp, H. K., and R. H. Yopp. 2000. "Supporting Phonemic Awareness Development in the Classroom." *The Reading Teacher* 54 (2): 130–43.

Index